WHEN THE

UNIVERSE

HOLDS YOUR

HAIR BACK

A Memoir by
KATIE BAKER

This book is a work of nonfiction. Some names and identifying details have been changed to protect the privacy of individuals. The events are recounted to the best of the author's memory and perception.

For information, permissions, or media inquiries, contact: hello@whentheuniverse.com

Cover design by KUHN Design Group | kuhndesigngroup.com

Photography by Marilyn Isaac Photography

Published by Peace & Fire Healing
Boise, Idaho
www.peaceandfirehealing.com

ISBN: 979-8-9928376-1-2
First Edition: June 2025

Printed in the United States of America

This book is dedicated to all survivors of childhood abuse.

I stand with you, holding vigil in the quiet places
where pain once lived. We are bound not by
what was done to us, but by the resilience that
carried us through. By the courage it takes to
heal. By the strength that is ours to reclaim.

You are not alone. You never were.

I see the triumphant spirit—the undeniable force within
us all—to rise, to break the cycle, and to reclaim the
power that was always ours. This book is for you.
For us. For the light that refuses to be extinguished.

AUTHOR'S NOTE

This book follows a mostly chronological order—as best as humanly possible—but each chapter also stands alone, like a short story. Why? Because I moved over 20 times as a kid, sometimes leaving a place only to boomerang right back, dragging emotional baggage heavier than my actual suitcase behind me. My mother was married five times and divorced four. Between the weddings and the court filings, there was a full spectrum of chaos and abuse; she had two biological children; my biological father had three. It's complicated. So, think of this less as a traditional memoir and more like a chaotic road trip where the GPS keeps rerouting, sometimes into oncoming traffic.

Also, names have been changed to protect the innocent. And the not-so-innocent got their names changed too. The last thing I need is a dead-beat stepfather crawling out of the woodwork to sue me. I already defeated those assholes in psychedelic ceremonies—I don't need one of them coming back for a second round.

AUTHOR'S NOTE ON MUSIC

Music was a vital part of my healing process. Each chapter includes a song that helped carry me through—though honestly, choosing just one per chapter was the hard part.

These are songs for the ones who survived what tried to break them.

Each track holds a thread of the story: grief, grit, healing, and hope.

Let the music carry what words couldn't.

To the artists who create such resonance, beauty, and transformation—thank you. Your music helped me come home to myself.

For more songs, visit the official playlist.

HEALING. HAIR-HOLDING.

Official Spotify Playlist

LEGAL DISCLAIMER

This book is a personal account of my year-long healing journey involving therapeutic psychedelics. It is not a guide, manual, or recommendation for others. The content is for informational and storytelling purposes only and does not constitute medical, psychological, or legal advice. Nothing in this book should be interpreted as encouragement or endorsement for the use of psychedelic substances.

My experiences are uniquely my own. I explicitly disclaim any liability for decisions made by others based on the content of this book.

Psychedelic substances and healing ceremonies can be powerful tools for transformation but also carry significant mental, physical, legal, and emotional risks. If you are considering exploring this path, do so legally, responsibly, and under the care of qualified, ethical, and experienced professionals. Research all applicable laws, risks, and integration practices before engaging in any form of psychedelic work.

Throughout my journey, I sought out legal settings and thoroughly vetted facilitators to ensure safe, supported experiences. With the growing interest in psychedelic healing, there has also been a rise in unqualified practitioners who may endanger vulnerable individuals and undermine the legitimacy of this work. Please exercise critical discernment when choosing a guide or setting.

I fully support scientific research and responsible, intentional use of these medicines, but I emphasize that psychedelics are not a quick fix, and their effects are highly individual. If you are considering this path, consult trusted professionals who can help ensure your safety and provide proper preparation and support for integration.

By reading this book, you acknowledge that any decisions regarding psychedelic use are entirely your own and that I assume no responsibility or liability for your actions, choices, or outcomes related to the content of this memoir.

CONTENTS

CHAPTER 1

I'M NOT OKAY

am a survivor, yes—but surviving doesn't mean escaping untouched. None of us make it through life without lasting scars.

A couple of years ago, the first thing I felt every morning was shame. Before my feet even touched the floor, it was already there—like a worn-out suitcase I had been dragging through life for years. Shame was my constant companion: my unwanted travel buddy. It followed me to the mirror, its weight bearing down on me with familiar, biting whispers: *You're a loser. An addict. A drunk, just like your father. You'll never be good enough—you never have been. You don't deserve this life. You're a waste because you can't even get it together for one single day.*

I was despondent, disconnected, and so detached from my emotional body it might as well have been on vacation. I didn't see myself as a victim, but I certainly acted like one. For years, I silently swallowed mistreatment, never voicing a complaint. I moved through the world as if I were less than—and people responded in kind, mirroring the lack of worth I failed to see in myself.

Anger, resentment, and disgust took root—not just toward the world, but also toward myself. I became a walking eggshell—fragile, cracking under the weight of it all, and impossible to put back together.

I was ashamed of the beer I drank—cheap, bottom-shelf beer which tasted like regret. I drank it for years, not even bothering to dress it up with the pretentiousness of a craft beer. It reminded me of growing up poor, a constant echo of a life I didn't want to live but couldn't seem to outrun.

In our family, drinking isn't just a habit, it's a tradition, woven into the fabric of every gathering, celebration, and ordinary evening. It's our identity, something we normalize, celebrate, and revere. We take pride in our ability to drink anyone under the table, seasoned pros in the sport of competitive drinking. Purple, wine-stained teeth? Those are trophies. A relative so drunk they need to be carried to bed by a sober grandchild. That's not a cause for concern—it's a highlight reel for the next day's jokes.

I come from a long lineage of drinkers; a legacy so deeply rooted it felt etched into my bones. It is an inheritance I never questioned but carried with dysfunctional pride.

I was mortified by the use of nicotine, the cigarettes that were both a crutch and a curse, leaving behind scars I could feel but couldn't see. I felt ashamed of my weight, each pound a physical marker of the pain and self-loathing I kept hiding.

And death? It was a shadow that clung to me and a quiet companion I had learned to expect. I almost welcomed it, convinced that cancer or some other reckoning for my choices was already written in my fate. I believed I deserved it—that this was the price for years of neglect, for the way I had abandoned myself, long before the world ever had.

Every weekend was a bender—an endless cycle of excess. Alcohol, cigarettes, food: it was like I was stockpiling indulgence, convinced the world might end by Sunday night. But the world never ended. Monday always came, dragging the weight of my choices behind it. And by Friday, I'd do it all over again.

It wasn't a celebration; it was a trap. My personal version of *Groundhog Day*, playing out the same scenes of self-destruction over and over. And each time, I thought to myself: *I don't want to live like this anymore. But do I even want to live at all?*

The physical struggles were symptoms of deeper battles raging beneath the surface. Weight gain, emotional eating, drinking too much: they were all signals of an attempt to numb what I couldn't confront. I hid in the sweetness of cookies, as if they could shield me or help me disappear. Discomfort clung to me like a layer of skin, a reminder that refusing to face the truth had heavy consequences.

Avoiding self-care wasn't an isolated problem—it was the gateway to every other destructive habit, creating an endless, exhausting cycle I couldn't seem to escape.

My childhood was defined by instability and exposure to the darkest sides of humanity. Alcoholism, sexual, physical, and verbal abuse, a lack of parental protection, and even brushes with the hardest drugs imaginable became my reality. I built the foundations for a survival-focused adolescence on these experiences when I learned to "buck up," endure, and strive for a level of perfection that was both suffocating and unattainable.

The message from my mother's expectations was unmistakable: keep pushing and keep up appearance no matter the cost.

Over the years, I mastered the art of appearing "normal," even convincing therapists I was perfectly fine. "*How are you today, Katie?*" they'd ask. I'd list updates, hold back tears, and skillfully steer the focus onto them. I became so adept at this that I paid qualified therapists to share fascinating stories about their own childhoods.

In my childhood, my mother had that one mantra: "Buck up." It was the cowboy creed of our household, a silent directive that shaped our lives: Don't feel—just do. Push through. Pull yourself up by your bootstraps and move forward. It demanded a level of emotional repression that buried feelings so deep that even my subconscious lost track of the toxic sludge building within me.

To her credit, "Buck up" had its advantages. It kept me out of prison. It taught me how to compartmentalize, to detach from pain, and survive. But at 48 years old, while walking the dogs, I had a startling realization: I had been so trained by this tough-love mantra that I no longer knew how to feel. My bottled-up emotions had either disappeared or imploded.

In the end, what I had built for myself was an emotionally bankrupt life.

Humor was my anchor, the lens through which I made sense of life's chaos. No matter how absurd, I could always find a way to laugh. But then the laughter disappeared. Smiles became a performance, a way to blend into conversations rather than a reflection of real joy. The humor that had once softened the edges of life was gone, and without it, everything felt unbearably sharp.

With my husband, children, and me, the absence of laughter isn't just silence—it's a void, a stark reminder that we're adrift, unmoored, and disconnected from what truly matters.

To the outside world, my life looked like a success—wise children who had sidestepped teenage rebellion, a loving husband, financial stability, and a career fueled by passion. But no matter how much I accomplished, something was missing.

When someone offered me a kind word or compliment about my work, my demeanor, or a heartfelt note of gratitude—I felt the words land, but they never sank in.

"You're amazing. Thank you for everything."

I'd smile, nod, say, "Oh, of course," but inside, I watched those words fall flat, heavy and lifeless, never making it past the surface.

It wasn't that I wanted to dwell in the past, I just never stayed there long enough to sift through the wreckage and salvage even a scrap of healing. Instead, I did what I was told: keep moving, keep pushing forward.

I followed the script society handed me—buck up, deal with it, don't repeat the cycle. I graduated from college. Got married. Had kids. Built a life.

Move forward. Deny what's behind you. Don't look back.

Happiness felt like a set-up, something I couldn't trust. Joy carried an unseen danger, a fragile illusion always on the verge of shattering. The weight of that fear had been with me for so long that it drained me completely.

I kept telling myself I was fine, as if saying it enough times would make it true. But I wasn't okay.

One day, I stood at the kitchen sink, mindlessly scrubbing a plate that was already clean. My hands were moving on autopilot—scrub, rinse, repeat—busywork to quiet the gnawing emptiness in my chest. The hum of the dishwasher, the rhythmic ticking of the clock: it was all just background noise to the storm brewing inside me.

I didn't notice my daughter at first. She lingered in the doorway, with her arms crossed, and her face wore shadows.

'Mom,' she said softly. A pause. 'Can we talk?'

I turned, dish towel still in hand, giving her my usual half-attention, the kind I had perfected over the years. "Of course, honey," I said, forcing a smile. "What's up?"

She shifted on her feet, her voice quieter this time. "You're not really here."

The words landed like a gut punch, stealing the breath from my lungs. I blinked, searching for her face, wanting her to say something different—to take it back. But she didn't.

"You're always somewhere else," she continued, her voice tight with frustration, maybe even hurt. "Even when you're here, you're not. And sometimes, I wonder if… maybe it would be easier for you if I weren't around. That way, you wouldn't have to pretend anymore."

I dropped the towel. The weight of her words crushed me. She wasn't wrong.

I wasn't living. I was moving through the days in a haze, devouring chores and drowning in work, hoping the busyness would suffocate the hollowness inside me. I had convinced myself that if I just kept going, checking things off my never-ending list, the ache in my chest would disappear. But she saw through it. She saw the exhaustion in my eyes, and the way my smile never quite reached my face anymore.

When I talked about my work, I had seen the flicker of concern in people's eyes, the hesitant pauses in conversation, their silence screaming louder than words. They could see it, even if I couldn't.

This wasn't a life of joy. Because it wasn't life at all.

And my daughter—my beautiful, perceptive daughter—had been the only one brave enough to say it out loud. From the outside, I might have appeared like someone who had it all together. But my family, as close as we are, saw through the carefully constructed facade.

Behind closed doors, they held gentle interventions—pushing me back toward myself through honesty, connection, and love.

My husband, a gentle and kind soul, grew up in a rough household, never fully realizing his own potential. His parents were hardworking but struggled to make ends meet, sometimes bouncing checks just to cover his school lunches. Life didn't offer him a roadmap out—no encouragement to break the cycle, pursue college, or even imagine a different future. He was left to find his own way, in a world that never made it easy. Our daughter entered our lives when I was 26—a determined firecracker with an unshakable inner compass, forging her own path with certainty. Our son moves to the beat of his own drum, navigating tough conversations with the ease of a trained therapist and thinking independently when it comes to societal norms.

Together, the four of us are a blend of distinct traits, each bringing complementary gifts, unwavering love, and a closeness that reverberates. We are each other's champions, biggest fans, and the first to call out one another's bullshit when honesty feels too heavy to carry alone.

One evening, not long after the conversation with my daughter, my son quietly pointed out how exhausted I seemed—that my constant pursuit of perfection was wearing me down. His words stayed with me, another mirror I wasn't quite ready to face.

My children and husband had seen my pain; it was no longer something I could keep hiding. A chance reconnection with a childhood friend unearthed stories of abuse I had locked away—brought up in casual conversation as if they were nothing. But they were everything. A visit with my biological father sent shockwaves through me, unraveling emotions I wasn't ready to face. A family member's suicide cast a long, unshakable shadow, pressing in on the walls I had built to keep the past at bay.

A collection of brutal, undeniable moments—they had always been there, arriving in increments, quietly ignored, skillfully evaded. But this time, they weren't just lingering at the edges of my awareness. They demanded a reckoning.

I wasn't just aware of them now—I was standing on the tracks, watching the freight train hurtling towards me. The railcars of repression stretched for miles, a lifetime of buried truths thundering forward, unstoppable. I could no longer outrun it. The whistle blew, the train was coming, and there was no escaping the impact.

And so, I broke.

The tears came, raw and relentless, as if a dam had finally burst. It wasn't just the weight of honesty that undid me; it was the flood of facing too much, too fast—years of suppressed truth rushing in all at once, demanding to be seen, and to be felt.

I was wrecked—this time, no amount of rationalizing or sheer willpower to pull me through. Overweight, over-drinking, overworked, and drowning in memories, I had been clinging to a fragile mantra: *I'm okay.* I could handle anything. Emotions were for the weak. Breaking down wasn't an option.

So, I pretended. Every day I convinced the world—and myself—that I was capable. *I'm not weak. I'm not soft. I can handle this.*

I had told myself those things so many times, but for the first time, a quiet voice inside me asked: *What if I am soft? And what if that's okay?*

I poured everything into work—at home, at my job, in every corner of my life. Even when I gave myself permission to heal, I stayed locked in the relentless rhythm of *doing*, running from the silence that might have forced me to *feel*. Because self-inflicted wounds don't always look like scars. They come in subtler forms—overworking, hiding, and numbing.

We can be our own perpetrators. Our own abusers. And the damage we inflict on ourselves can be just as brutal as the wounds left by others.

I had buried my pain so deeply that I didn't want to know what lay at the bottom. It was so dismal that I feared I'd never find my way back to the surface. The dark nights of the soul piled up like a never-ending rerun of a TV series, forming a scrapyard of despair that was nearly impossible to escape.

Over the years, there had been fleeting moments when I reached for something beyond indifference. The moments had been rare, a fragmented marathon of effort that left me breathless but resolute. I knew I couldn't keep ignoring the call to heal myself.

There's a dread in telling my story—an apprehension about looking between the hidden cracks, scraping away the caked-on grime I convinced myself was just the past. I told myself it didn't matter. I was an adult. It was forgotten.

But through the lens of my life, I saw the truth: salvation wasn't found at the bottom of a 16-ounce tallboy or a whiskey glass. I had walked that path, tested it, and found only a dead end. I tried talk therapy, meditation, yoga, and exercise, all the things that should help. None of them did, I was just too far gone.

I had spent years numbing, ignoring, outrunning the past—convincing myself that if I just kept pushing forward, I could outrun the hungry ghosts that followed. But the past doesn't just disappear. It waits.

No amount of self-help strategies, meditation, or neatly packaged wellness routines could touch the wounds I carried. I needed something deeper. Something more. So, I decided that I would change everything.

I committed to a year of healing, determined to work with therapeutic psychedelics—not casually, but with the same unrelenting, take-no-prisoners attitude that had defined my survival. My children's words echoed in my mind, forcing me to confront the stark reality: my life was emotionally barren. I had been running on fumes, clinging to the last scrap of effort I had left. Something had to change. There had to be another way.

It was a last-ditch effort to save myself.

I thoroughly researched every medicine before I ever took a single dose. I immersed myself in preparation, reading books and articles, listening to podcasts, diving into *How to Change Your Mind* by Michael Pollan, and seeking out personal experiences from seasoned psychonauts.

Every four to six weeks, I plunged into another ceremony, barely integrating the last before throwing myself into the next. I approached psychedelic healing the only way I knew how—relentlessly, with sheer force of will, hoping that if I pushed hard enough, I'd finally break through.

But I learned quickly: healing isn't a battle to be won. It's not about conquering—it's about surrendering. The lessons came hard and fast, exposing the way my old habits—control, resistance, and endurance were no longer serving me well.

Month after month, I boarded a plane to the place where these medicines were accessible, immersing myself in ceremonies with ayahuasca or a powerful combination of MDMA and psilocybin. Each journey pulled me deeper into the unknown, forcing me to confront the parts of myself I had long avoided.

This book is about courage. About vulnerability. About creating connections for those who see their own wounds reflected in mine. It is a book about giving voice to the unspoken, about breaking the silence that trauma forces upon us.

Because healing belongs to all of us.

Before the year officially began, I eased into the journey with a small dose of mushrooms in a serene garden with a trusted friend— just enough to dip my toes in before fully diving in. I was cautious, afraid that a higher dose might unravel me completely.

The idea of peeling back the layers—of facing what lay beneath— felt overwhelming. So, when I first sat with psilocybin in a garden, guided by a well-versed friend, we chose the daytime. The darkened sky felt too intimidating, too heavy.

That was the moment when the dark figure approached. I heard sticks snapping beneath the weight of its steps. Its presence loomed— unmistakable—even through the safety of the eye mask I wore. It hovered at the edge of my vision, a shadow I could almost make out beneath the fabric. My friend suggested I walk through the garden, and so I did. But the figure remained—a mystery, a question left unanswered.

The figure disappeared, but I knew it wasn't gone. It was waiting. And six months into my journey, it would return—with answers.

That day, however, something shifted. I saw life through a new lens, the intricate dance of insects moving with precision, the way the leaves whispered in the wind, and the gentle surrender of the fading sun.

I hadn't lost my mind.

I had begun to find it.

A year of deep healing gave me the opportunity to finally face the parts of myself I had long avoided. Putting it into words felt vulnerable and terrifying, yet it was also another step toward becoming whole. For years, I had found solace in glossing over my past, hiding behind distractions, or escaping altogether. I didn't begin this journey in crisis—but after four decades of emotional, spiritual, and physical disconnection, I inevitably hit rock bottom.

And it wasn't loud or dramatic. It was quiet, crushing, and utterly demoralizing. A whisper—*Help. Please help*—so faint I almost missed it. A fragile plea from deep within me, one I barely had the courage to acknowledge.

The moment my son said, "Mom, we can all see that you're struggling," it ignited a personal revolution. What followed was a year of healing—both beautiful and brutal. A journey that unraveled me, stripped me bare, and rebuilt me in ways I never could have anticipated.

Little did I know, the very substances I had been conditioned to fear would become the ones to set me free.

I suffered the greatest damage in my life from the legal drugs— alcohol and tobacco, among others, not the illegal ones. And yet, it was the "illegal drugs" like psilocybin, MDMA and ayahuasca that became my unlikely guides. Walking me back home to myself, helped me navigate the shadows of my pain, and carved a path toward wholeness.

My goal was simple but daunting: to face the truth of my life with complete honesty. For as long as I could remember, detachment had been my shield against emotions too heavy to bear. Vulnerability felt foreign—like scaling a mountain without a map. But deep down, I knew it was the only way forward. I had to turn inward, no matter how uncomfortable.

The journey was neither linear nor comfortable—it was messy, unpredictable, and relentless.

It was filled with starts and stops, breakthroughs and breakdowns, and moments of clarity followed by plunges into the unknown. Sometimes it felt like I was unraveling the fabric that held me together. I faced the darkest corners of pain.

I drank the medicine, and the shadows of abusive fathers rose before me—silent, looming, and daring me to finally face them. Not just them: there was also the wreckage they had left in their wake. I saw everything I had spent a lifetime avoiding—my perceived failures, my limitations, and the truths I had ignored. Healing wasn't just about shedding the weight of my past—it was also learning how to exist beyond it.

Facing the truth of my life required an intervention—a path I hadn't anticipated, one I didn't fully understand and wasn't sure I wanted to take. Some of my family members had been working with ayahuasca long before it was "cool." Honestly, the thought of it tripped me the hell out. I wasn't just afraid of drinking the medicine—I was terrified of what it might reveal. What if the skeletons in my closet weren't just ghosts of the past, but monsters lying in wait, ready to drag me under?

I had listened to their wild jungle adventures with a cocktail of skepticism, doubt, and resistance. Over 25 years ago, they were paddling canoes through the Peruvian Amazon, sipping plant medicine, and unearthing spiritual breakthroughs—while the rest of us were surviving "Livin' La Vida Loca", organizing floppy disks, hoarding Beanie Babies, and preparing for Y2K like it was the end of days.

They were the eccentric ones—diving headfirst into the mysteries of the universe, while I stayed firmly grounded in the conventional norms of Western culture. I was raising babies, checking off my to-do lists, and trying to hold everything together rooted in the belief that stability came from structure, not from drinking something brewed in the middle of the jungle. I always took their stories with a grain of salt—and a raised eyebrow. I thinly veiled my concern, wondering what on earth they were trying to discover out there in the jungle.

I had spent 20 years knowing therapeutic psychedelics existed, but I had been brushing them off, convincing myself I didn't need a psychedelic intervention. But what if I was wrong? I had nowhere to go but up. The same thing I had dismissed, even feared, might hold the key to the healing I had been searching for my entire life.

Exploring the stories of my childhood might be dark, but it wouldn't just be a tale of pain and trauma—it would be one of hope, redemption, and salvation. The light I eventually found—the one we all deserve—came only when I stopped running and faced the experiences that had shaped me. They didn't define me but were woven into my journey. They had all left a mark on who I'd become.

Returning home to myself was messy—sometimes mortifying and cringeworthy—but it would be a success story against all odds.

The journey was long and heavy—a slow trudge through darkness before glimpsing the light. Healing is never truly finished. Life unearths new layers, throwing curveballs just when you think you're through. Truths resurface, refusing to be ignored, and demanding to be faced and freed.

Letting demons run my life was bottom-of-the-barrel, shit-crew labor for the brokenhearted—a slow surrender disguised as survival. Facing them? That took courage. I was convinced that I was tough but sleepwalking my way through existence wasn't strength—it was avoidance wrapped in bravado.

I was living a life veiled in weakness, pretending to be unbreakable.

Of all the stories that make up my life's scaffolding, this one is worth telling—not because it's perfect, but because it's *real and painfully raw.*

"FACE DOWN IN THE MOMENT"

Nathaniel Rateliff & The Night Sweats

CHAPTER 2

THE BOOGEYMAN

M y childhood trauma exhausted me, so I tucked it away in a nice, neat little box, pretending it didn't exist. There was just too much fatigue and anguish tied to it. For years, I ignored it, sealing it shut with a pretty little bow.

Like I shared earlier, in my 40s, the box unraveled on its own. The bow came undone—tired of waiting, reminding me it had never truly disappeared. With my children growing up and leaving the nest, the signal was clear: I could finally allow myself to fall apart. For the past 20 years, I devoted myself to building a secure, loving home for them—a deliberate contrast to the instability of my own childhood. I did the job of mother with maniacal determination.

Now, the box opened; one corner at a time, the box's contents were exposed. Like a jack-in-the-box, every version of me up to the age of 20 stood there, waiting for me to heal them. From the age of 20 to 47 years, I had been dead inside—going through the motions and failing miserably at leaving the past behind.

As an adult, I told the stories of my childhood. But it lacked emotion, as it was reduced to facts. I recounted memories like cautionary tales about the boogeyman. I'd tell people, *He's real, he's out there*. And I believed that warning, because I had seen him.

The boogeyman lived inside our homes, stole the souls of little children in every town. I knew him well—he had haunted every home I lived in. He crept through the floorboards, whispered from the darkness of shadows, and left his stench on everything he touched.

He wasn't a mythical figure, summoned in a mirror with a candle during a sleepover. He wasn't an illusion or a ghost. The boogeyman was human. Worse, he was someone I knew.

The boogeyman wasn't a shadowy figure hiding under the bed. He was a child molester. An abusive alcoholic. A rapist. A priest. A troop leader in a church that concealed their sins. A family member— a father, stepfather, and someone's brother. He was flesh and blood, he lived among us, and his self-serving cruelty left scars that never faded. The scars of abuse had burned entire villages to the ground.

In the end, he grabbed me, and his hands tightened around my throat as he spewed venomous words in my ear. When words weren't enough, his grip tightened and choked the light from me until I believed every lie was the truth.

I knew the devil by many names. He held the box in his hands, daring me to finally face him—to defeat the darkness and save all the versions of myself still trapped inside.

"THE JOKE"
Brandi Carlile

CHAPTER 3

PURPLE TEETH, CROWN ROYAL AND SALVATION

The fire pit blazed six feet high, sending sparks spiraling into a night sky so wide it swallowed everything. Around me, the familiar signs of another Labor Day reunion: the slap of cornhole bags, drunken howls of laughter, the sharp pop of a beer tab cracking open. I was fifteen beers in, trying to disappear into the noise, when my son dropped down beside me, silent for a long moment, his face lit by the flickering fire.

"Mom," he said, his voice steady, cutting through the haze, "we can all see you're struggling. Maybe it's time you take a year for yourself. Maybe it's your turn now."

I didn't know it then, but his words would split something open inside me—the beginning of a slow, messy, necessary undoing. It would take Crown Royal, purple teeth, a battered heart, and an unexpected kind of salvation to find my way out. But first, like every year, we had to make it through Prineville.

At their core, Labor Day family reunions are a living tapestry of American family dynamics—stitched together with admiration, heavy slugs of booze, deep-seated dysfunction, and everything in between. As tradition dictates, every year, my parents, our children, my husband, and I embark on the five-hour pilgrimage from Idaho to Oregon, winding our way toward Prineville—a gathering we affectionately called a family reunion, but is more of a rowdy frontier spectacle, a debauchery-laced homage to roots in the Wild West.

Two-lane highways unravel before us, flanked by weathered barns adorned with oversized American flags and declarations of patriotism, fading in the high desert sun. Each small rural town we pass feels like a forgotten relic, where time slows, and the scent of alfalfa and diesel lingers in the air. It's a journey not just across state lines, but into the heart of family lore—where the past and present collide in a whiskey-soaked embrace.

The air is thick with the unmistakable scent of sage and juniper, a fragrant reminder of familial roots stretching deep into the high desert soil. The landscape shifts, signaling the family ranch is just around the bend.

When we pull up to the back of the ranch, we are met with the usual warm welcome: drinks in hand and bear hugs that squeeze the air out of your lungs. My aunt's joyful laugh rings out as she walks toward us, my uncle chimes in with a casual, "How was the drive?" and family friends gather around, ready for the inevitable hug procession.

Arriving here is like a weekend in Vegas. You start off brimming with hope, energy, and a sense of fortune waiting to be uncovered. But there's also a nagging awareness that by the end, you'll be drained, broke, and hungover under the scorching desert sun.

Prineville boasts dive bars, staple restaurants, a modest courthouse, and the quintessential small-town vibe. My family in Central Oregon dreams of joining Idaho through the Greater Idaho initiative—a long shot, yet a testament to their deep-rooted frustration with "big city folks," a sentiment that never seems to fade.

My cousin Lola works at the diciest dive bar in town, a place where time stopped in the 1950s. Decades of use make the appliances hum, the chairs creak untold stories, and the bare walls carry layers of smoke-stained memories from a bygone era.

On Saturdays before noon, we make our pilgrimage to this relic of a bar, lining up to take shots, cheer on football games under a sprawling American flag, and get real with the locals. These are the folks who start their day with a stiff drink at 10 a.m., sipping liquid courage alongside their morning coffee. It's here that the town's pulse beats the strongest—raw, unvarnished, and authentic.

We enter the bar and are greeted by shouts of "Yello!" echoing through the room. The townies are awaiting our arrival to shake things up. My 18-year-old nephew presents Lola with a hat that reads, "Hawk Tuah 2024, Spit on That Thang." Only Lola could pull that hat off. She strikes an "owning it" pose, flashing the biggest shit-eating grin while the family watches in a mix of amusement and pride.

Lola is the cool cousin who seems allergic to seriousness. At the family ranch, she's the type to sneak stolen White Claws to slightly too-young cousins, shotgun Red Bulls for "convenience," and when boredom and booze collide, suggest impromptu leg-waxing sessions.

"Motherfucker!" or "I'm *sweating and* I'm *spitting!*" becomes the soundtrack of the leg-hair-removal project as the family gathers around the firepit. It's all hands-on deck, and somehow, amid her pain and profanity, it's bonding.

Lola's father, my cousin Champ, is not "quite the character," but *the* character. With his deep, low radio voice, a full head of blonde hair, and outfits so colorful they could rival a music festival goer or a Parrothead, he is a presence you can't miss.

One year, the family gathered for a weekend of wedding prep for another cousin's big day at the ranch. People filled the dance floor, creating a packed and lively reception buzzing with energy. Champ, never a man for dramatic flair, but aware of a crisis when he saw one, marched to the microphone, cutting off the music mid-song. You could hear the album scratch across the speakers.

With a booming voice and the gravitas of a news anchor delivering breaking news, he declared, "FOLKS, WE HAVE AN EMERGENCY!" There was a slow pause as the crowd turned their rapt attention, "WE ARE OUT OF BEER! THE KEG IS EMPTY!"

It wasn't a mere announcement—it was a dire proclamation. The slow dance grounds to a halt, with guests frozen and looking around in disbelief. There had to be at least 40 people there, and they hadn't just drained one keg—they had powered through two.

As panic rippled through the crowd, they called in favors and got a third keg in route. Only then could the song resume. Meanwhile, my uncle muttered something under his breath about *Jesus* and *how this could have happened*, shaking his head like we'd just watched a pirate plunder our last keg, leaving us stranded and dry.

Of course, we strategically outsource our family drama to a select few for maximum efficiency. It's the nuttiness that makes you question why you braved five hours of sketchy country roads, packed on five pounds from all the beer, and endured five too many rounds of bullshit. They burn hot, tucker themselves out with tire-screeching theatrics, and then make a grand, dramatic exit—leaving the rest of us to raise a beer in relief as they tear off like *The Dukes of Hazzard* down the road.

The women may be short, but we're scrappy—a feisty little junk-yard lot, just the way God intended. One year, my mom decided she'd had enough of the chaos and started yelling things like "THAT'S ENOUGH!" or the classic "I'VE FUCKING HAD IT!"

We wanted to believe her threats, but her wine-stained, grape-juice purple teeth destroyed any authority she attempted to project. Try as we might, we just couldn't take her seriously—not with those purple-stained chompers snarling back at us. Bless her heart, she really gave it her all, though.

At my family's place, the entire focus is on indulgent food, belly laughs fueled by storytelling, and a lively mix of family and towns-people. Six-foot-high fire pits crackle as a feral pack of dogs' weaves between our feet, scavenging for scraps. The property sprawls across five acres—with horse pastures stretching into the distance, pole barns standing tall, and three outbuildings ready to house the revolv-ing door of visitors.

My uncle, who ran a popular local restaurant for years, has turned their place into a culinary paradise, with barbecues, smokers, large outdoor fridges, and fire pits. There's no shortage of entertainment—corn hole, volleyball, miniature golf, frisbeer, and ring toss games keep folks occupied for hours while they sip on cold beverages. We alter-nate between energy drinks and good old American beer to ensure we have the staying power to party from dawn till dusk (and then some).

Every year, Paula, a lifelong family friend, graces us with her pres-ence, and over time, she's become an honorary member of the family. One particularly unforgettable year, we threw a 70s-themed retire-ment party for my aunt. The house was alive with disco music, glitter jumpsuits paying homage to *Saturday Night Fever*, striped tube socks, and tie-dye galore—it was a night to remember.

Paula, as always, brought her own distinctive flair to the evening. Just before a memorable encounter with a screen door, she attempted a sultry pole dance using a decorative light fixture. Unfortunately, her enthusiasm proved too much for the base, sending her sprawling onto the floor, tangled in the faux pole, with her fringed leather pants, vest, and 70s hairstyle disheveled. Trying to maintain some dignity, she handed me her drink and sighed, "Katie, can you please get me another drink? Mine spilled."

Taking her glass, I asked, "Sure, Paula, what do you want in it?"

"Just vodka, honey," she replied.

I stared at the pint glass in my hand, momentarily perplexed. "You want me to add ice?"

"No, Hun, just vodka," she insisted.

Later that night, Paula capped off her performance by mistakenly wandering into the wrong room at bedtime. In her confusion, she declared it her own, ejecting a sleepy child unceremoniously from "her bed." Her antics ensure there's never a dull moment, and for that, we are grateful.

Then there was the infamous year when about eight men crammed into the jacuzzi, tossing their beers directly into the water for "simple beer drinking." For three hours, they sat there, chatting and laughing, but something was amiss—none of them had gotten out to use the bathroom. Not once.

By midnight, I decided I'd had enough and scurried off to bed, leaving my husband, Dean, out there with the crew. At some point, he dozed off, somehow keeping his head precariously above the water.

The next morning, the hot tub told the entire story. The once-clear water had turned an unsettling shade of green, and it took little detective work to figure out the cause. It was a collective *contribution* of urine from the night's festivities.

My Aunt Sadie took one look at the scene and made an executive decision: the hot tub had to go. "It's too dangerous," she declared with absolute seriousness, adding, "We have to keep Dean alive."

And that was the year the family hot tub met its untimely demise, sacrificed in the name of health, hygiene, and—most importantly—the preservation of Dean's life. The thought of him drowning in a bubbling cauldron of pissy water, surrounded by half-empty cans of warm beer, was a collective nightmare none of us wanted to realize. Even Dean agreed it was a headline best avoided: *"Visiting Family Member Found in Hot Tub Horror."*

Then there was the year Dean, and a family friend had a Crown Royal drink-off. Spoiler alert: it was a terrible year for both. But it gave us enough laughter and ammunition to last the next three years and gave us the inspiration for the theme of the family T-shirt the following year.

Jax, a weathered, 70-something legend of a man—revered for his toughness and no-nonsense attitude—challenged Dean to a drinking contest. Dean, who isn't cut off from Prineville cloth and doesn't drink hard liquor, never stood a chance. I don't know if anyone technically "won" the contest. In fact, it's safe to say they both lost.

Full-blown alcohol poisoning incapacitated Dean the next day, and Jax's intoxication was so severe that four people had to load him into his camper. At one point, he decided to "take a piss," and promptly fell out of the camper, leaving his head with a battle scar. As we tried to stuff him back in, someone suggested we get his pants off to avoid a future urination mess because pants would be a liability.

The morning cleanup offered yet another gem: a pair of dentures lying casually next to the firepit. Apparently, in the evening, Jax had grown weary of his false teeth and decided the firepit was the perfect resting place for them.

And that is why Crown Royal and hot tubs are now banned from family gatherings.

Aunt Sadie and Uncle Joe are the hosts of the festivities. Though unrelated by blood, Sadie is family in every sense—our matriarch. Her father was a horse whisperer long before the term became famous, a wiry man who spent his days at horse camp, with a pipe dangling from his lips, sharing quiet wisdom by the fireside.

Sadie is a straight shooter, known for calling things as she sees them—the only exception being if it hits too close to home. She'll stop a political debate mid-sentence and, if she says it's done, we accede out of deep respect. When she bows her head to say grace before dinner, her deep devotion to the family often overwhelms her, and her voice falters, bringing tears to everyone at the table. It's a poignant reminder of the love and fragility that holds us together, even in the face of our imperfections.

Sadie is the embodiment of hospitality, with an unshakable cowgirl grit and the unofficial title of the World's Best Bloody Mary Maker. Uncle Joe is a quiet man, content to sit back and observe. He's a rock of stability but not without a tender side—every so often, the beers loosen his reserve, and deeper conversations bring a mistiness to his eyes.

I remember asking him once what his favorite job had been in his lifetime. Without hesitation, he replied, "When I was a logger." There was simplicity in his answer that struck me, yet it seemed profound. Logging for him—and for many others in the family, including my grandfather, wasn't just work. It was a connection to the untamed beauty of the forests, to a sense of camaraderie and peace that seems almost mythical in today's fast-paced world.

In those forests, I imagine they found something rare: a clarity of purpose, a connection to nature, and the serenity that comes from honest labor. There's a longing in that reflection, a wistful nostalgia for a time when life was more grounded, with its meaning woven into the daily rhythm of hard work and community.

The family's personality medley is a mosaic of mental illness, political clashes, personal struggles, and no-nonsense gutter talk. As the beers flow, so do the expletives—delivered liberally, with flair, and always with high expectations. They endearingly refer to a standard 12-oz beer as a "little baby bitch beer," and a 16 oz Pabst tallboy as a "no fucking around beer."

And yet, beneath all the silliness and boisterous banter, love and acceptance somehow rise to the surface. If we can hold on to that patience—no small feat in all the chaotic personalities, a quiet confidence emerges that no matter what, we can survive it all. Affection, shared history, and an enduring sense of belonging connect our messy family, however tattered it may be.

As much as I once resisted it, I accept the town—and my family—as a part of my heritage, and thus a part of me. It's a legacy I can't deny, and one I've learned to carry with equal parts, reverence and humor. But over time, I've come to appreciate my embodiment of both worlds. I'm a shit talker with a tough streak but also, a city-dwelling upstander driven by a sense of justice.

When the pandemic hit, the spirit of the town was on full display. During the Prineville protests in the summer of 2020, people rode down Main Street on horseback, guns locked and loaded, making it clear they would always protect themselves. It's a place where loyalty runs deep, and being well-armed is a rite of passage.

The Labor Day reunion tradition began the year my grandpa passed away. We all converged on Prineville to honor a great man—a lumberjack by trade and a veteran by life circumstances. A man of quiet dignity, Grandpa wore a flannel shirt, jeans, and suspenders. He was reflective, exuding a confident strength. There was a tough quality about him, paired with a sense of loving awareness that was often discouraged in the era that raised him.

We overcame the drama and sadness of that weekend and continued the family reunion tradition for 15 years after his passing.

One year, my grandpa's lovely wife, Marge, joined us for a family outing to the newly legalized cannabis dispensary. In her 80s, and as dignified as ever, Marge gamely loaded into the family minivan along with as many relatives as could cram inside. We rolled up to the store, driver's licenses in hand, ready to see what we might be missing out on.

Grandma Marge, however, stayed behind in the car with my husband; neither had any interest in the family shenanigans. When we emerged with brown bags of potential (and a little shame) in hand, there was Marge, sitting patiently with her perfectly coiffed silver hair and wrinkle-free outfit, the picture of composed elegance.

As we loaded back into the car, she turned to my husband and said with her characteristic poise, "I haven't smoked pot yet, and I'm not planning to soon." Still, she'd come along, squeezing into the clown car packed to the brim, offering her unwavering support for our peculiar little mission.

During my childhood, my cousin Knox was our constant sidekick. In our bloodline, it was just me, my brother, and Knox. He was cowboy-strong and a wild child, a magnetic force of energy and charm. He grew into a towering figure of a man, with shoulders that even Zeus would envy and a grin so devilish it could charm the pants off any woman within a five-mile radius.

Knox had an uncanny ability to turn our world upside down in an instant—one moment, it was fun and games, and the next, he'd threaten someone's life over a minor disagreement. The realization that Knox could genuinely hurt someone wasn't just a passing fear; it became a sobering reality. Over the years, we all tried to maintain a connection, to find glimpses of the cousin we'd grown up with. But inevitably, we'd retreat in silence, licking our wounds, unsure if we could endure another round.

Yet Knox was also the life of the party in his moments of light. I vividly remember one family reunion where he decided it would be a great idea to raise me on a forklift, perched on a pallet in the pole barn so I could dance. My fear of heights turned it into a glorified safety dance, swaying nervously while Knox egged me on. When they finally lowered me to solid ground, I experienced exhilaration and profound relief. That was Knox—pushing the limits of both joy and chaos in equal measure.

Then came the year when a distant cousin, Finn, came for Labor Day. Unfortunately, he had an undiagnosed mental illness, fueled by alcohol, which contributed to the already combustible family mix. After the usual beer-guzzling ritual, Finn picked a fight with Knox. Physically, it was no contest—Finn was welterweight at best, while Knox was pure heavyweight, a Kermit-the-Frog-vs-Thor matchup.

As if provoking Knox wasn't enough, Finn inexplicably escalated the situation by whipping out his penis in front of the crowd, adding a surreal twist to an already absurd confrontation. A collective chorus of "*Oh no!*" and "*What the actual fuck*?!" escaped our mouths as we turned to each other with bewildered expressions, silently asking the same question: *Who does that?*

Naturally, Knox responded in the only way Knox knew—with his fists—pummeling Finn as his exposed anatomy flopped around in the chaos. Somehow, Finn escaped, sprinting to a neighbor's house where he breathlessly declared his life was in danger, and promptly called the police.

The night's events had drawn the entire family into the "Scooby-Doo mystery" of the dick-slinging, ass-kicking fiasco by the weekend's end, with each of us piecing it together.

That weekend, Finn had taken it too far—even for our family, and that's saying a lot. In a clan where mayhem was practically a birthright, Finn had outdone himself, crossing a line none of us thought possible.

Years later, Finn spiraled further downward, mixing street drugs with severe mental illness. Knox, too, eventually descended into the depths of mental illness. On the weekend of Grandpa's funeral, he beat his stepbrother Brent so severely that he spent the weekend hiding in the house, bruised and bloodied, probably lucky to be alive.

Earlier that same night, Knox had convinced my husband, Dean, and my brother to join him for a drunken round of ball-hitting at the golf course. Their escapades had left them too drunk to drive the truck, so they naturally stole my uncle's golf cart for their triumphant, albeit slow, return. The golf cart, traveling on the 55-mph highway, could only have reached 15 mph.

Our wide-eyed disbelief met their triumphant expressions when they finally rattled into the driveway, grass-stained and grinning ear to ear.

They paraded my uncle's golf cart down the highway like a victory lap. "It seemed like a good idea," they all said, nodding in drunken solidarity, as if their logic made complete sense. My uncle shook his head and walked back into the house.

Despite the chaos, Knox brought moments of love and laughter, but the darker tendencies overshadowed it. When we didn't side with him in a family argument, Knox called later, threatening to have us "go missing" with the help of his friend Hippie. Moreover, when he stayed at our house, things would simply go missing—cologne, tools, money, the list goes on.

Each of us tried to help Knox reach the potential we had glimpsed before mental illness tightened its grip, warping him into someone we no longer recognized. But in the end, we walked away defeated, our efforts shattered, our hope swallowed by the storm.

The loss crashed over us like a relentless wave—not just grief for who he had become, but mourning for the person he had once been. There were family reunions where my stomach knotted with unease, as I scanned the trees and bushes, afraid he might be lurking, and waiting. The way he cut ties with people wasn't clean, it was jagged, uneasy. There were moments when I feared we might not make it back to our home state.

Family gatherings were the original battleground.

Reunions meant returning to the root base of our family tree which kept our feet entrenched in the same old patterns. The vibrant fall leaves outside reminded us that change was a possibility, but inside, we clung to limited belief systems. Who needs personal growth when you can just stick to what you know? Like an unwelcome guest, our behaviors and patterns clung to the sadness of a half-lived life, as we pretended everything was fine.

Every year, we gathered to share and revisit countless stories—a testament to our resilience or, perhaps, our stubborn refusal to let go of the past. Alcoholism? Acceptable, even encouraged. It was during these gatherings that I learned how to cowboy up, brush the dirt off my shoulders, and lean into the infamous fortitude that comes with our family name. The fortitude was a birthright, passed down like an unspoken code for survival.

When I projected toughness, I didn't feel a damn thing. In our world, crying was for the weak. Vulnerability? A luxury we couldn't afford.

The only time it was acceptable to crack—to let the sadness seep through, and to show even a glimmer of brokenness—was when we were drunk. Only then could the softer side emerge, as our raw underbellies were briefly exposed from beneath the armor we wore daily.

Otherwise, we didn't show weakness. We didn't ask for help. We just kept going.

Our family did not discuss difficult topics. But the problem with ignoring the hard stuff, the unaddressed issues, was that it didn't disappear. It lingered, simmered just below the surface, until it eventually erupted.

So, we toasted cheap beer, each sip an unspoken plea for a better place in life. We consumed copious amounts of alcohol, edibles, or whatever vice, feeling both stagnant and small—like that stubborn piece of corn stuck in your teeth that just won't budge. Between wild games of corn hole on meticulously crafted boards, we forgot about "growth" while watching a relative unleash a stream of angry rhetoric about the state of the world after devouring the evening news. It's a slow-motion train wreck we couldn't look away from.

We morphed into the Vegas version of ourselves—a love ride filled with the heights of laughter and the lows of addiction. In one day, we felt everything: loved, tiny, and completely overwhelmed. By the end of it all, I wasn't sure whether to laugh, cry, or just reach for another drink.

We mourned the passing of family, hosted self-righteous debates that made family therapy look like a picnic, and stolen golf cart highway drives that were more thrilling than a rollercoaster. We had created soul wound scars and borne witness to the despair of mental illness, along with alcohol poisoning so fierce it required a 24-hour recovery period that rivaled a hangover retreat. That's not to mention the random dentures left at the base of the fire pit in a fit of drunkenness—because nothing says "family reunion" quite like a set of teeth resting by the flames. Yet, despite all the chaos, we returned every year as if it was the only way home to a clearer sense of belonging.

The night by the fire with my son marked a turning point I didn't see coming. I had been spiraling—mentally, emotionally, spiritually—and thought I was doing a decent job hiding it. But my son saw right through me. His words didn't just land; they cracked something open.

For years, I had carried the weight of survival so quietly that even I forgot how heavy it had become. But sitting there, wrecked and exposed, my son offered me something I hadn't known I needed: permission. Permission to unravel. Permission to heal. Permission to let someone else hold the weight for once.

My son never dances around the truth.

"You've had a really rough childhood. I don't even know how you survived it," he said. "You've done such an incredible job raising us. But maybe now… maybe now it's time to focus on yourself. Take a year to heal yourself. We'll be okay, Mom. We've got you. It's your turn now."

I sat frozen, his words hitting me with a force I hadn't expected.

For so long, I had buried my truth under layers of resilience. Now, it was all laid bare.

I muttered something about trying therapy again, but even I didn't believe it would be enough.

He didn't blink. "We know you've tried everything," he said. "What about ayahuasca or something like that?"

That moment—his clarity, his love, the unflinching mirror he held up—was the first spark of something new. It was the beginning of the beginning.

Looking back, that night was more than just a conversation. It was a sacred rupture. A moment where the truth, long ignored, demanded to be seen. And it was my son—my child—who delivered it with grace and clarity. The torch was passed, not in duty, but in love.

As a mother, it was strange and deeply unsettling to realize that my greatest fear wasn't my suffering, but the possibility that my children could see it. I hated the idea that they might recognize how lost I was and see how much ground I was losing. His clarity and compassion felt like a wake-up call, both comforting and heavy. Under the warmth of the fire and the chill of vulnerability, I understood—perhaps it was time to face my scars instead of hiding behind them.

My son's words cut through my carefully constructed veneer of "okayness." His clarity and compassion struck me like a wake-up call. In that moment, I realized I had done what I set out to do; I had successfully guided my children into adulthood. They were strong, wise, and ready to stand on their own. But what about me? Somewhere along the way, I had abandoned myself—left "me" behind, scattered across the years. Was it when I was a toddler, a young child, a teenager, or even an adult? Or maybe all the versions of me had been missing for so long, they belonged on the back of a milk carton.

It became painfully clear that something had to be done. That conversation didn't just illuminate the path forward; it demanded that I take the first step.

Alcoholism was the respectable family vice, disguised as humorous camaraderie and tradition. For generations, drinking had been how we coped, connected, and celebrated. But for me, it had become a numbing agent, a ritual to quiet the exhaustion and evade the ghosts. This ghost whispered to me, urging me to drink another beer, eat another edible, and drown myself. Instead, I sat, remaining vigilant, witnessing my fatigue, "honoring" it through the nightly ritual of dulling every sense that I had available. Beer had become my escape, providing a temporary reprieve that kicked in by the second drink, each sip an attempt to forget.

That single conversation with my son under a vast sky full of stars became a turning point—a moment that permitted me to change, and to confront what I had been avoiding. My son and daughter, wise beyond their years, had both seen my truth with a clarity I could no longer deny, as if they'd looked it up in Webster's Dictionary and found the definition in plain sight. His words broke through the thick armor I had worn for years. I grasped the power of being seen and faced myself for those I loved.

As I said, I had family members who had ventured deep into the Amazon to drink ayahuasca, seeking peace and wisdom. For years, I had dismissed it as indulgent, woo-woo nonsense. But as I sat with my son's suggestion, something shifted. *Could there be something to it? Could this sacred brew offer what therapy hadn't—relief, understanding, healing?*

My son was right, it was my turn. The time had come for me to explore the depths of my darkness, heal the wounds I had spent a lifetime hiding, and uncover who I was. The path ahead felt uncertain, layers of performative strength, but I knew I had to start somewhere. I formed a plan—a way to step into the light, one deliberate step at a time. I didn't know this at the time, but the plan would begin with psilocybin, followed by ayahuasca, sacred tools I had once dismissed as indulgent.

As I embarked on my "year of healing," I gathered up my emotional baggage and stepped through the only open door left to me. This wasn't going to be a neat journey with tidy resolutions—it was messy, painful, and transformative.

"A PRAYER OF MY OWN"

Nick Mulvey

CHAPTER 4

THE SHADOW OF FATHERS, THE LIGHT OF BROTHERS

The first time I met my brother, Tommy, he was 35 years old, and I was 49. His foster home sat in a rough part of Salem, Oregon, a modest house with chipped paint and a chain-link fence that barely contained the worn-out yard. The air smelled of damp pavement and distant fast-food grease, and the hum of traffic was always present in the background.

Tommy was standing on the porch when I arrived, wearing a red hockey team shirt, his brown hair shaved close, and short facial hair giving him a scruffy, almost boyish look. He was sweet, kind, and funny in a way that immediately disarmed me; his presence radiated a warmth that made it impossible not to smile.

His foster mom introduced us with a simple sentence that changed everything:

"This is your sister, Katie."

Tommy stopped in his tracks. His entire expression shifted, his eyes widening with genuine surprise. He turned to me, repeating the word "Sister"—slowly, and deliberately, as if testing its weight, as if the very word had the power to reshape everything, he knew to be true.

And then, with the purest joy, he hugged me. Not just any hug—one of those rare, all-consuming embraces that make time stop. He clung to me as if this newfound discovery was the most extraordinary thing in the world, and he had waited a lifetime for this moment.

After a long, quiet beat, he pulled back just enough to place one hand over my heart while resting the other on his own. His touch was light but intentional, his eyes searching for mine with an openness so rare it nearly took my breath away.

"Good heart," he said simply.

Something inside me split at the seams. His words lifted a weight I hadn't even realized I was carrying. No pretense, no hesitation—he saw through me, right to my core.

I understood something profound: this was family, stripped of expectation, history, or resentment. Just two good hearts, meeting and recognizing each other for the first time.

My father Buck had two sons, Billy and Tommy. Tommy was born when I was 14 years old, under hushed tones within the family. He was born with Down's Syndrome and a congenital heart defect that would demand extraordinary care and love. Between the years, and the distance with my father, I never met Tommy.

I don't recall how my grandmother reacted at the time of Tommy's birth, perhaps with quiet sadness. But my grandfather and father chose to bury their heads in the sand, pretending Tommy didn't exist. It was said that both my father and Tommy's mother, Loretta, were drinking heavily at the time of Tommy's conception, and rumors played into the blame game.

In my father's eyes, all the blame rested squarely on Loretta's shoulders. In the rare moments when he mentioned Tommy in the early years, it was only to emphasize Loretta's heavy drinking, as if that explained or excused his own absence. That was his way—placing the entire burden of raising a beautiful, vulnerable child with complex health needs solely on her shoulders. It was always his way: escaping responsibility when things got hard.

I spent part of my summer months with my biological father's parents in Oregon—relishing the sense of normality those visits provided. I felt deeply connected to my grandmother, despite having little communication with my biological father. But Grandma Betty's warmth and stability were a lifeline. I would leave the chaos of Prineville behind and step into her quiet, white house with its covered front patio, where she welcomed me with open arms, as if I had always belonged.

Grandma was stunningly beautiful. Her streaked silver-gray hair framed vibrant blue eyes, the kind of effortlessly beautiful gray that people now pay good money for at a salon. A slight hump in her back bore the weight of years of hard labor, a testament to the life she had lived. She had raised eight children, and carried the burdens of a well-worn life, yet her strength was woven into everything she did. She was one of the greatest forces for good in my life.

During my visits, we were inseparable. We baked cookies, made dinner, and tackled painting projects to cover up the nicotine-stained walls. And in those quieter moments, we sat at the kitchen table for hours, pretending to read the newspaper—more interested in simply being together than in the words on the page.

Often, it was just the two of us—sometimes joined by her best friend, Mauve. Together, they exuded an effortless cool, the kind that the teenage me—trapped in the awkward purgatory of braces and breakouts—desperately hoped might rub off.

By contrast, Grandpa was a man of few words. After his shift at the wood mill a mile away, he'd shower, take his seat at the kitchen table, light a cigarette, and quietly nod along to the conversation. Everyone knew he was a professional philanderer, but Grandma Betty tolerated him with a quiet, simmering disdain. Their conversations were clipped and transactional, revolving around the day's newspaper, while I sat awkwardly, waiting for the moment I could escape the tension hanging over the table.

Back then, he'd line up for government cheese and whatever else was being handed out. He'd return home with the haul—thick blocks of orange cheese wrapped in plain packaging. To this day, that cheese lingers in my memory as some of the best I've ever had. Maybe it was the novelty of charity, or the way it gathered us around the table, but in an otherwise modest life, it felt like a small, unexpected luxury.

His attempts at disguising his baldness were far less dignified. What little hair he had, he grew into an ambitious mullet, shellacking it into a stiff, upward wave with heavy-duty hairspray—and, quite possibly, super glue.

One morning, when Grandma asked me to wake him, I knocked on Grandpa's door. No answer. Cautiously, I peeked inside—only to be greeted by 1.5 feet of hair standing at full salute, frozen mid-lightning strike.

Panic surged through me. I bolted to tell grandma that grandpa had been electrocuted in his sleep. She laughed so hard she could barely catch her breath, tears streaming down her face as she gasped for air, trying to reassure me between fits of laughter. When she finally composed herself, she sat me down for the *faux-hair-toupee talk*, explaining the secrets behind Grandpa's towering masterpiece. To this day, I can't look at a can of hairspray without remembering that moment.

Most of her eight children launched into success, but a couple, including my father, never quite got off the ground until I was in my late 20s.

Even after my summer visits ended, I kept in touch with Grandma. She was wise, honest, and never one for small talk. Our phone calls were about the real stuff—the kind of conversations that are rare and hard to find.

I remember the first time she told me she had met someone new. I was still reeling from Grandpa's passing, expecting her to sound lonely, or maybe even resigned. Instead, there was something light in her voice, an almost girlish excitement that I hadn't heard before.

"Oh, Sis, he makes me laugh and I just feel good," she said, and I could hear the smile through the phone. She always called me "Sis" or "Sister," a term of endearment that carried the weight of unconditional love. To honor her, I've carried on that tradition, calling the best women in my life "Sis." It's my way of celebrating the profound truth she taught me—that we are all part of the same tribe. There's a unique power in that bond, a shared strength that helps us weather life's storms together.

The idea of Grandma Betty finding love in her 70s felt radical to me. It struck me how many people saw older women like her as an afterthought, as if their purpose had already been fulfilled. But Grandma had never been one to live by others' expectations; she had taken her fill of life, and she wasn't done yet.

Years later, as I neared the end of my 20s, a mother of two—I felt a gnawing urgency to call her. It had been a month since we last spoke, and guilt sat heavy on my chest. Life had a way of stretching time between calls, but this time felt different. I could feel her absence like an unspoken pull, a tether tugging at my heart.

Finally, I climbed that hill of guilt, sucked it up, and dialed her landline.

"Well, hello there, Sis!" She greeted me, her voice as warm as ever.

That call turned into the most beautiful hour-long conversation about life, death, and everything in between. Her health was stable, aside from her worsening glaucoma, but there was an eerie resolve in the way she spoke—like someone who had already made peace with the inevitable.

"I've lived a full life, Sis. I've loved deeply, raised my family, and had a full life. I'm ready for the pearly gates."

I spoke to her on a Friday.

She broke her hip on Saturday.

And by Sunday, she visited God.

Looking back, I knew she knew. She knew it was our final call, and we said our goodbyes with love.

Whenever I feel lost, I think of her and the unwavering belief she had in our sisterhood. And I found my way home.

During that final call, my grandmother had gently pleaded with me to reach out to my father.

"Your dad has quit drinking," she said. "I just want to see you two rebuild something before I go."

After she passed, it felt like a debt I couldn't ignore. She had provided me with so much security and love during those summer visits—the least I could do was try.

So, I began reaching out. Despite how unsettled I felt after every interaction; I tried.

The phone calls and visits never brought comfort. Most of the time, my father would launch into a rambling rant about someone who had wronged him, or his general frustrations with the world, displaying a complete lack of accountability for his own choices.

It was never about me.

Ninety-five percent of our conversations were me listening to him—a one-sided symphony of self-pity and bitterness. I endured it out of obligation, and out of love for Grandma, but after everything I had suffered in childhood, I often hung up furiously. This happened more times than I care to admit.

Before I was born, my mother faced an impossible decision. She ended a pregnancy, knowing that bringing a child into the chaos Buck created would mean condemning them to a dark and uncertain future. I often wonder how that choice sat with her—if it haunted her in quiet moments, or if she wished she'd found the strength to leave him sooner.

I survived the womb despite his rage—despite the drunken punch he aimed at my mother's pregnant stomach. That act of violence, directed at a life yet to begin, was the final blow that drove her to leave him. It wasn't just her safety at stake anymore, it was mine.

With nowhere to go, my mother turned to an aunt, who took her and her unborn child into their home. The choices she faced—abuse intertwined with alcohol—must have been terrifying. I came close to being another casualty of his destruction. So, I am lucky to be alive.

When my mother remarried when I was one, my biological father opted to have my stepfather adopt me—not out of love, but to avoid child support. He was problematic, to say the least; after the adoption, it became painfully clear that my brother and I had different fathers. We had been raised in the same house and I never quite felt like I belonged the same way my brother Mike had.

I didn't want to be different. I craved belonging. But having different fathers created an invisible divide, a double life I had never asked for. It left me with an overwhelming sense of isolation, like a puzzle piece that never quite fits: almost, but never fully, a complete part of the picture.

I remembered my first memory of meeting my father when I was about six years old. He was a stranger, a shadowy figure appearing for the first time in a park in Oregon. The word *dad* felt as foreign as he did. He wasn't a presence in my life, he was more of a shadow, a fleeting figure who left only the wreckage of his choices in his wake.

By my 20s, he had become a sad caricature, the kind of person you might read about in the back pages of a seedy human-interest story. His excessive drinking had cost him his wife and daughter, and some of my worst memories of alcohol could be traced straight back to him.

Buck is built like a logger, with a barrel chest and soft eyes that hint at a quiet, reflective nature when sober. He carries himself like a man born into the wrong century, someone who might have thrived navigating the rugged western terrain, clad in animal fur and ready for battle.

When I was young, he retreated to the remote wilderness of Alaska, chasing some romanticized vision of a fur trapper lifestyle. For me, an animal lover by nature, this was just another strike against him, a growing list of reasons why I viewed him as irredeemable.

I would receive postcards or letters postmarked from Alaska; each one written in a voice that didn't quite feel like his. It was as if he were impersonating someone else—perhaps a fellow fur trapper tempting to forge a connection. The words felt hollow, the kind of ramblings that only isolation and boredom can conjure. I could almost feel the loneliness bleeding through the ink; each letter was a stark reminder of the quiet madness Alaskan isolation can foster.

Reading his letters felt like stepping into a scene from *The Shining*—a remote cabin, endless solitude, a slow unraveling into something unhinged. Who knows what horrors unfolded deep in those woods, but the words he sent were enough to make me shudder.

"Sorry I didn't write earlier. I have been really busy."

Later, the letters would drift into the mundane—details of long, empty days spent watching for mountain goats. Or, worse, a plea to my single mother:

> "I'd like to be able to send less money. I barely have enough
> food. Hope you understand that it's hard for me."

It was a glimpse into his world—one of self-imposed exile, desperation and detachment.

I remember those letters, a stark reminder of the reality he so often glosses over. Maybe even Alaska couldn't offer the escape he'd always been chasing.

Once, when I was about ten years old, I remember sitting stiffly on the cracked vinyl seat of the city bus, with my small hands gripping the metal pole for stability. The rhythmic hiss of the hydraulic doors opening and closing was the only steady thing about the ride. Beside me, Buck was already drunk—his breath thick with beer, his eyes unfocused but still burning with the misplaced anger he always carried. I couldn't tell you if he had been drinking before our outing or if he had smuggled a flask in his coat pocket. It didn't matter. The result was always the same.

At first, he seemed fine. Slouched in his seat, shifting restlessly, the way men like him always do when they've lost control of everything but still feel the need to dominate a space.

Then, the bus driver made the wrong move. Maybe he braked too hard. Maybe he said something Buck didn't like. Whatever it was, I felt the shift before the first word left his mouth.

"What the hell kind of driving is that?" Buck slurred, his voice slicing through the bus like a dull blade.

I froze, my stomach clenching into a hard knot.

The bus driver didn't respond, eyes locked on the road, but Buck wasn't going to let it go.

"I said, what the hell kind of driving is that?!"

Heads turned. Passengers stiffened in their seats. I kept my gaze locked on the floor, wishing I could disappear into the dirt-streaked rubber mats. Maybe if I stayed small enough, no one would associate me with him.

But he wasn't done.

His voice grew louder, and uglier. And when the bus driver still didn't take the bait, Buck's anger turned—like a snake changing targets mid-strike—and suddenly, it was about Grandma.

"You know what? My own mother thinks she's so goddamn special, sitting up in her little house, thinking she's better than everyone else!"

The breath left my lungs.

It wasn't just that he was drunk and belligerent—it was that he had turned his venom on the one person in my life who had ever made me feel safe.

I gripped the edge of the seat, willing myself not to cry, or to react at all. I knew better. Reacting only fueled the fire.

His words spilled out like poison: slurred insults about the woman who had raised him, the woman who had taken me in during the summers and given me moments of normalcy. He mocked her, degraded her, and dragged her name through the dirt right there in front of strangers.

The bus rumbled on. No one said a word. I could feel people staring—pitying and embarrassed for me—but no one intervened.

When the bus finally reached a stop near our destination, I shot up before Buck could, darting down the aisle and out of the doors as if I was escaping a burning building. In a way, I was.

I didn't wait for him on the sidewalk. I didn't slow my steps. I just walked, fast and far, my face burning with shame, my hands balled into fists.

I don't remember what happened after that. If he caught up. If he even noticed my silence. But I do remember the promise I made to myself that day—

I will never be like him.

I will never let alcohol turn me into a monster.

And I will never, ever tolerate someone speaking of my grandma that way.

Back in the days before caller ID, answering the phone after 4pm was like playing Russian roulette with my sanity. Every ring was a gamble; if I lost, I'd be met with the slurred wrath of the man who had given me up for adoption yet still felt entitled to my presence.

Even after years of his drunken tirades, after he had branded me a perpetual people-pleaser, I still answered his calls. Through my teenage years, I endured his verbal lashings, the venom he spewed at the world, and the drunken monologues that were more about his suffering than any semblance of fatherhood.

But by the time I reached 18, I was done. Burned out.

Even then, college didn't free me from him.

He would call my dorm, demanding to speak to "the cunt just

like her mother." Sometimes, it was just "cunt," as if my bewildered roommates were somehow responsible for summoning me.

I still remember the look on their faces—raised eyebrows, hesitant glances, a half-whispered, "Uh... I think your dad is on the phone. He's... asking for the cunt?"

Mortification.

I'd grab the phone, cheeks burning with humiliation, pressing it to my ear as if I could somehow absorb the shame before it spread further into the room.

And then it began.

If he wasn't already belligerent, he was on his way there.

Sometimes, I'd have to calm him down, talking to him like he was a bomb about to detonate. Other times, I just had to sit there and take it—a full hour-long tirade about how the world, women, coworkers, and even the server at his last meal had all wronged him.

Every word dripped with bitterness, a mirror of the resentment he carried toward life itself.

I thought, *maybe if I'm patient, if I show him kindness, he'll change. He'll see me. He'll love me.*

But at 19, that illusion was finally shattered.

One morning, after a drunk tirade the night before, I called him back.

I don't know what I expected—an apology, an ounce of regret, or maybe, just maybe, a sliver of acknowledgment that he had done damage.

Instead, he sighed, bored.

"I've had a rough life," he said flatly. "And you just need to get over it."

Just like that.

I sat there, the receiver still pressed to my ear, staring at the wall as his words settled like cement over my chest.

No matter how early in the day it was—whether he was sober or barely drunk, words of remorse or accountability would never cross his lips.

That was all I needed to hear.

I didn't speak to him for ten years.

For ten years, silence was my shield. Then, out of love for my grandmother, I found myself dialing his number—knowing full well that some distances can never truly be bridged.

But the emotional weight was an endless cycle of frustration and disappointment. No matter how much I spoke to him, the distance—both emotional and physical—remained insurmountable.

He was never a father to me. He was never there for me. Just a name on a birth certificate, a shadow I spent years trying to reconcile.

Meanwhile, there was Billy—the brother I barely knew, 23 years younger than me. He grew up in the same small town, living with my father and his mother. Buck wanted us to have a relationship, but blood alone couldn't unite siblings. The gap between us had been carved long before we ever had the chance to know each other, shaped by the man who connected us in name but never in love.

Unlike me, Billy had been born healthy and male—the only qualities that seemed to matter. His mother and my father stayed together for a few years, but their relationship unraveled, and they eventually parted ways.

Despite the separation, my father remained in Billy's life, raising him the only way he knew how—through hunting, fishing, and collecting antique weaponry.

Billy was always the golden child, the perfect son my father had always wanted. I didn't resent him for it, but I did feel a quiet sadness for him, whether he recognized it or not. His birth wasn't just an event, it was a declaration of perfection in my father's universe, a role that came with an unspoken, crushing weight of expectation.

Billy allowed me to exist in relative peace and quiet, untouched by my father's pressure.

We saw Billy periodically as he grew up, but the turning point came at my grandma's 80th birthday celebration. That was the day he crossed a line that I could not ignore.

During the event, Billy, a teenager, took it upon himself to educate my young children on how to find inappropriate content on the internet. Later, when I caught them exploring exactly what he had suggested, I pressed them for the truth. Not only had he encouraged it—he had even recommended specific websites.

That was the moment when I knew Billy needed far less access to my children.

From that point on, whenever my father tried to arrange get-togethers, I found myself making excuses, pushing the visits further and further out of reach. The truth was, I had no interest in playing family with people who didn't respect my boundaries.

Besides, my father hated city driving, which meant any visit required traveling to some small Oregon town where I would have to play along with the illusion of connection. And quite frankly, that was an effort I no longer cared to make.

Phone calls from my father were predictable—either stories about Billy or complaints about his job at Union Pacific. One of his routes brought him through Idaho; occasionally, he'd call to suggest meeting in Nampa, just 30 minutes from where I lived. He'd offer lunch, and when we met, the routine was always the same: a greasy diner and an antique shop—his preferences, never mine.

Our visits were never about getting to know me. They were honoring his requests, making him feel at home, and catering to his comfort. Despite years of phone calls and sporadic visits, he never really knew me.

Like any one-sided relationship, it could only last so long. Eventually, I realized it was time to pull the plug on the energy vampire he had become. But it wasn't simple. There was still that lingering sense of duty—the weight of trying to be the daughter he had abandoned so long ago.

I had promised my grandmother I would try. But in the end, I saw the truth: I had spent years trying to be a daughter for him, while he had never once tried to be the father I needed.

The calls from my father took on a different tone as Billy got older—an edge of distress crept into his voice. He'd mention how Billy had stayed out all night, sleeping all day, and running with the wrong crowd. Call after call, it became clearer that Billy was spiraling. My father, ever in denial, brushed it off, but I knew addiction when I saw it.

I tried, in the gentlest way, to make him see the truth. He wouldn't accept it. Not yet. It took years before reality became undeniable—by the time my father finally accepted his son's failure, Billy had dropped out, fathered two (or possibly three) children before turning 20, and the weight of it was dragging him under.

He gravitated toward women who mirrored his own struggles—girls with rough backgrounds, dropouts, or addicts, the kind who spent their days lost in drugs and video games. Eventually, he moved into a house where there were no rules, no structure, and no one to stop him. It was the kind of freedom that comes with chains.

I urged my father to push him into the world, to get him out of the small-town rut before it swallowed him whole. For a moment, there was hope. Billy graduated high school and even enrolled in a few college classes. But the change didn't stick. Sobriety came too late. And death, in its cruelest form, came knocking.

From what I've gathered, the mother of his child broke his heart. Desperate to numb the pain, he returned to old habits, taking a dose his body could no longer handle. By morning, they found him— Billy, drugs laying by his side, was unresponsive on the floor. He was 20 years old.

My father called to deliver the horrible news. Anger and sadness swelled within me as I made plans to attend the funeral of a brother I hardly knew. The loss felt like that of a stranger—a blood connection that had been severed before it ever truly existed. Through my interactions with my father, I sensed an untold story, a missing piece of Billy's life that I would never hear from him. It was too late. And once again, I felt like the only child of a father I never really knew.

The funeral was suffocating and not just because of the grief hanging thick in the air, but because of the murmurs from townsfolk— whispers of how the town had lost too many of its young people to opioids. It was a tragedy in small towns so common that it had become a new normal.

The addiction, the spiral, and the slow-motion wreck Billy had become—it had all been there, plain as day. But it was too late.

Billy made his own choices. He had free will. But my father's stubborn refusal to face reality left me with an ache—a deep urge to shake him, to make him see what had been so painfully obvious.

I did what was expected. I went through the motions—paying my respects, nodding politely, and listening to the eulogies.

The grief came from the weight of accumulated loss, of watching the same patterns repeat, and failure that ran like a fault line.

And now, there was no fixing it. No redemption. Just the empty act of getting through another day.

Much later, during my year of healing, I read an article about my father saving a family who had driven off a bridge into the river below. I felt a rare flicker of something—pride, maybe, or disbelief. The story detailed one of the few truly heroic acts I had ever known him to do, a stark contrast to the man I had come to know.

A grandfather, driving with his wife and two grandchildren, had fallen asleep at the wheel. In a rare moment of courage, my father jumped into the water to save them. *The Oregonian* wrote a glowing article about his heroism, celebrating him as a man of action, of bravery.

Around that same time, I visited a psychic medium, not expecting much, just curious. But as we sat together, she mentioned something that made me pause. "Billy is with you," she said, almost offhandedly, as if stating a simple fact. "He was there while you were reading that article."

Her words jarred me. I hadn't thought of Billy at that moment, and hadn't felt his presence. But the idea that he was watching—quietly, unseen—stuck with me.

I found myself rereading it, as if trying to reconcile the man in the article with the one I had grown up knowing. It was strange, this duality—how someone could be both a savior and a destroyer, both a rescuer and a man who had left wreckage in his wake.

Later, another intuitive echoed the same sentiment. She, too, sensed him near, but this time, there was no message. She gently asked him to *move along*, as if acknowledging his presence while also letting him know he didn't have to stay.

But it was the third intuitive who gave me an explanation that settled into my bones. She told me that *as I healed, he was healing too.* She said that our father had wounded him, just as he had wounded me. Maybe, as I unraveled the damage within myself, Billy was finding some kind of closure on the other side.

It all clicked.

I had spent so much time wondering why he lingered near me, why he would choose to watch over a sister he barely knew in life. But I had been looking at it the wrong way. It wasn't about the relationship we had. *It was about the healing we both needed.*

The irony is, I feel closer to Billy now—after his passing—than I ever did while he was alive. In some way, he needed me to heal just as much as I needed to heal. Maybe the traumas of his short, complicated life had tethered him here, unfinished, and unresolved. And maybe, through my own healing, I was helping him untangle those knots, too.

The thought brings me a strange kind of peace, the realization that healing doesn't just move forward, but backward too.

I've read countless stories, references, and books about those who cross over yet remain tethered to the living. And I believe there's truth in it. If we don't face our emotional baggage, addictions, or traumas in this life, they don't just vanish, they follow us. Maybe into the next life. Maybe into the lives of those we leave behind.

I choose to believe that.

For me, making this life as right as possible feels like the safest bet. I don't want to leave behind unresolved failures, heartbreaks, or wounds—only to have them resurface in another form, in another time. I'd rather face them now, head-on, when they rise up demanding to be seen.

And in a strange way, Billy's lingering presence became a reminder of that. We are all connected in ways we don't fully understand, and healing isn't just an individual journey—it ripples across generations, across lifetimes, even for those who are no longer here.

After Billy's passing, my father stepped in to take part-time care of his children. Their mothers, already lost in their own storms, were barely staying afloat, making an already heartbreaking situation even heavier.

It's been painful to watch—children fight battles they never chose, wounds etched into their lives by the cruel patterns of addiction—patterns that started long before them, and that they never asked to inherit.

And so, the cycle continues, endlessly repeating itself until someone, somehow, finds the strength to break free.

It's rare, but some manage to liberate themselves from the weight of a legacy that keeps dragging them back. But most aren't so lucky. They're swallowed by the same struggles, the same demons that haunted their parents.

Watching Billy's kids makes me think of that every time—the fragility of it all: the cycle, the struggle, the desperation. How easily can a life be steered toward the same wreckage without anyone even realizing it.

In his own way, my father is trying now. Maybe it's too late for Billy, but he's doing what he can for his grandkids, stepping in where he can, and trying to make things right in the only way he knows how.

And while our relationship remains fractured, while the years of damage still cast their long shadow, I acknowledge his effort. But it doesn't erase the past. It doesn't undo the hurt.

But maybe, for once, he's finally showing up.

For my father, this is significant progress. He may not have been able to save Billy, and he certainly failed both me and Tommy in countless ways, but his effort with Billy's children feels like the closest thing to redemption he may ever find.

I don't know what the future holds for those children. The hill they must climb is steep, and the odds are stacked against them. But seeing my father step up in any capacity—despite everything—gives me a small shred of hope. Maybe this is his way of trying to undo at least a fraction of the damage he's caused.

It's imperfect. It might be too little, too late. But it's something. And sometimes, in the tangled mess of family legacies, "something" is better than nothing at all.

My father visits the same bridge every day, praying for my brother at the spot where a dragonfly is embedded in the concrete. There's something undeniably poetic about it, especially since this bridge is also where my father became a local hero, by saving that family.

Yet, as powerful as that story was, the article in The Oregonian conveniently omitted the messy truths. There was no mention of Tommy, my other brother, whose very existence my father had ignored. I was reduced to half a sentence. No mention of the years of absence, the neglect, the damage that could never be undone.

The article honored my father's heroism and mourned the loss of Billy—his life, his absence, my father's grief. And I didn't mind. It painted the picture my father wanted the world to see—the man he wished he had been all along. And maybe, in his mind, that was enough.

But what did bother me was what came next.

One day, I confronted him. I told him the truth, the one I had carried for decades—the ways he had failed me, the wreckage he had left behind in my childhood. I wanted acknowledgement, some scrap of accountability. But all I received was a deflection. He pivoted, telling me about his own childhood wounds, how his parents had moved from Sisters to Bend, Oregon, which had been deeply traumatic for him.

I had overcome sexual, verbal, and physical abuse. He had barely survived a change of zip codes.

I sat there, silent.

That conversation was a turning point. Something shifted in me.

I called my daughter afterward, feeling drained and hollow. She asked me three simple questions:

> *"Do you love your father?"*
>
> *"How does he make you feel?"*
>
> *"Does he deserve you?"*

The answers came effortlessly.

> *"No. No. And NO."*

It was like a light inside me quietly flickered off, as the room where I stored all my father's emotional baggage went dark. I had spent years carrying the weight of his absence, his failings, and his indifference. And suddenly, I realized I didn't have to anymore.

Fourteen months into my healing journey, I met with an intuitive for four hours—yes, four hours. One of the most profound takeaways was this: *let him go.* She told me my father was doing me more harm than good, so my energy needed to be redirected elsewhere. She said, *"You have a brother. And he is kind. And funny. He is someone you should invest in."*

A week later, I made the first move. I asked my father for Tommy's mother Loretta's phone number. It was small, but it was a step.

When I reached out to Loretta, I didn't know what to expect. She answered in a weakened voice and told me she was in a hospice. I cried. It just happened that I had found her in the last week of her life. She cried too—because Tommy had a family who cared about him.

I canceled my weekend plans and booked a flight, determined to get to her before it was too late. But I didn't make it in time. My flight was on Friday. She called me Thursday morning to tell me she wouldn't make it to Friday.

Tommy had been placed in foster care because of his Down's Syndrome and heart defect. There was no one besides Loretta that could properly care for him. The doctors had once said he wouldn't live past ten, but Loretta had loved him for longevity—feeding him organic food, letting him watch *Barney* on repeat, holding him in the unconditional embrace of a mother's devotion. The heartbreak in her voice was visceral. She was dying before he was, and she knew it.

On our last call, she told me she remembered me as a child, that I had always been a wise soul. Then she told me something that would set me free.

"The healthiest thing you could ever do is live free of your father."

For years, I had held onto my grandmother's wish that I try to have a relationship with him. But after 49 years, I finally realized—I *had* honored her request. I had *tried*.

And now, it was time to let go.

The irony of it all was that my brother's mother—Loretta—was the one who set me free.

She never got to see me in person, but she knew I was coming. She knew her son mattered to me. And I hope that knowledge brought her peace, because at the heart of it, that's all a parent wants—to know their child is loved.

Through this journey, I realized that my father had cast a shadow over my life for far too long. But the love I found—with my brother, and with myself—was so much bigger than his absence.

I deserve better.

I choose better.

And I believe that, in healing myself, the ripples move outward, moving through time, through generations, through bloodlines that stretch far beyond what I can see.

For years, I wrestled with guilt over leaving my father behind. But after meeting Tommy and speaking with Loretta, I saw the truth: my father didn't even know that Tommy had been placed in foster care. His neglect was so complete that he had no idea his own son had been taken from the only home he had ever known.

When my father called, I calmly told him the truth. I told him I needed acknowledgment, accountability—something he was never willing to give. But I also told him that I was my own sovereign being, just as he was.

"You owe me nothing," I said. "But I owe you nothing, too."

And with that, I let him go.

Through the fires of healing, I reclaimed my bravery, my voice, and my boundaries. And I found liberation.

I had spent years tolerating harmful behavior simply because of a family blood connection. Shame, guilt, and an old, tired sense of obligation had kept me clinging to something that had never served me.

But in the end, I gained something far greater:

I met my brother.

We connected through our good hearts. And that was all the love I ever needed.

I finally found the missing piece.

And it was never in my father—it was in the sacred bond of unconditional love, in the resilience of a mother's sacrifice, and in the purity of Tommy's innocence.

Once, we were strangers, connected only by blood. But in the lightness of reunion, we found something greater—family, in the purest sense of the word.

"SOMEBODY'S CHILD"
Blessing Offor, Dolly Parton

CHAPTER 5

A ROOSTER: SERVED WITH A SIDE OF KARMA

After my mom escaped the wreckage left by my father, she remarried a roofer called Snake. His family ran a local roofing company—a legacy stamped on the side of a building, emblazoned on trucks, and splashed across glossy brochures. So, when I was just a year old, my mom and I packed up and moved to the Willamette Valley in Oregon. We settled into a cozy, single-story, three-bedroom house at the base of Long Hill. We had a cat named Isaac and held onto the illusion of the perfect American family. My mom and Snake soon had a son, Mike, completing the picture-perfect scene: boy, girl, two parents, and a pet cat.

This was the era of Strawberry Shortcake attire, *Little House on the Prairie* books, and my rad pink bike with tassels flowing freely in the wind. My mom sewed matching Strawberry Shortcake outfits for my best friend, Carrie, and me, and we often wore them around the block.

My brother and I, just two years apart, spent plenty of time beating the crap out of each other. During particularly rowdy playtimes, our parents would quickly confiscate the golf clubs from our surly little hands. We spent our days riding bikes around the neighborhood, walking to school together, and suffering relentless teasing from our cousins in the schoolyard.

While my brother tore around on his bike and Snake worked in the garage, creating beautiful stained-glass pieces and fixing whatever we broke, I often got lost in quieter pursuits. In our Oregon yard, I would spend hours captivated by fuzzy orange-and-black caterpillars, carefully building them ornate little homes from leaves, sticks, and water bowls made of acorn shells.

The late 70s and early 80s seemed like simpler times. After school, my friend Carrie and I would go over to her house for snacks, and to hide from her older sister. The initial bond between us was the shared dislike over Strawberry Shortcake's nemesis, The Purple Pieman. However, neither of us could deny that Purple Pieman plastic toys smelled heavenly. He was an evil guy with a creepy mustache, but in plastic, it smelled great.

My mom approached my biological father, Buck, about having Snake officially adopt me. Seeing it as an easy way out of financial obligations, my dad agreed. While I carried Snake's last name, it was clear he never truly saw me as his own.

One of my strongest memories is of Christmas with Snake's extensive family in the Willamette Valley, where we would gather at my new grandparents' house. We played basketball and explored the hidden treasures beneath their massive deck, where thick Oregon moss clung to the wood and bewildered deer watched us wild children run free.

For the holidays, my grandparents would set up a towering tree, sprayed blue with Rust-Oleum, for a touch of classic elegance. The presents stretched across the living room, stacked thoughtfully in every corner. The kids would tiptoe around the gift-laden room, scanning the tags for their names, only to erupt in excited shouts when they found one.

My grandparents' leather rocking chairs were like thrones, planted firmly in the middle of their modest living room. They practically lived in dark leather comfort during their free time, rocking steadily, as if the rhythm itself held them upright. I never recall them venturing far from those chairs. They sat there like two bookends, exhausted but steadfast. Years of labor had carved marks of strength and perseverance into their calloused hands. My grandfather, the quieter of the two, had returned from World War II and dedicated himself to building a business and a life in the community. He had founded the roofing company, working long hours to make it a success. By the time my brother and I arrived at their house on weekends or after school, the weight of their work exhaustion lingered in the air—unspoken, yet undeniable.

An oversized clock, looming like a silent overseer in the main entryway, filled the room with persistent ticking. Every hour, its chime reverberated through the house, a reminder that time trudged on, unhurried. However, from my childhood perspective, my grandparents' appearances showed no sign of passing time. My grandfather would lean back slightly with his jovial belly pushing over his waistband, and a slow smile creeping up the corners of his lips as he offered a soft "mmm" of acknowledgement when spoken to. My grandmother, in contrast, was a spitfire, quick with a look that meant pure business.

Her pink tiled bathroom shrine stocked an array of lotions and potions promising softness and comfort but rarely used. Grandma didn't exude high maintenance—her practicality was her hallmark. Still, there was one indulgence: her perpetually stubborn skin abscess the size of a ball tip pen. Nestled on her neck like an unwelcome tenant, it demanded attention.

"Katie," she'd call with a twinkle of mischief, "if Grandma paid you a quarter and a cookie, would you squeeze it for me?"

I would hesitate for a moment, considering the price. A quarter wasn't much, but the promise of another cookie from the jar holding our sugary salvation was worth the bargain. The jar sat temptingly on the counter, its cheerful face masking the gluttony it encouraged. My grandmother, reclining in her throne, would hand me the coin like a queen giving a favor.

After the "chore" was done, I'd retreat to the comfortable living room where my grandparents quietly sat, the rocking chairs creaking softly. The rhythm of their chairs, the tick of the clock, and the occasional hum of my grandfather's voice created a backdrop to my childhood—steady, comforting, and eternal, like passing time.

Every summer, us kids would pile into the car and head to Aunt Berna and Uncle Danny's house, where life always felt a little louder, a little wilder, and a whole lot sweeter. Each family member had their own quirks, but none were quite like my Aunt Berna.

She was the original fun, wild woman—a whirlwind of energy with short blonde hair, a couple of missing fingers, and a true zest for life. Zest for life coursed through her veins—she danced without music, toasted without reason, and carried a spark that could ignite an entire room.

She had a habit of calling her husband "yummy," and not in a passing, cutesy way. With the seriousness of a love-struck teenager, she'd grab your arm, lock eyes, and ask, "Isn't he so yummy?" The question, coming from a grown woman to a kid, flirted dangerously with the gross-fine line, but with Berna, it was impossible not to love her for it. She meant it with her whole heart, and that kind of devotion was rare enough to admire—even if it made you squirm.

I felt truly free when we'd pile into her black Trans Am, the wind whipping through the open sunroof as we screamed into the summer air—sugar-crusted Fun Dip sticks raised like tiny, neon-colored torches of rebellion and liberation. With the music blasting, Berna kept one hand on the wheel and the other firmly planted on her custom horn, a ridiculous, blaring announcement that she and the Trans Am were coming in hot. It was perfectly fitting that Berna had a musical horn that played different tunes—it was as wild as she was.

Every holiday, the house was transformed into a spectacle so extravagant that anyone within a 10-mile radius knew a celebration was near. Inside, we lived in a sugar-fueled paradise—candy at our fingertips, blue soda pops in hand, and the jacuzzi bubbling in the background. As we sipped our sodas, our eyes always landed on the quirky water fountain on the back patio: a child froze in time, urinating into a stream of unnaturally blue water. It was weird. It was wonderful. It was Berna.

We were quintessential 80s kids, high on sugar and freedom, running wild through a house that felt more like a circus than a home. And in that chaos, we belonged.

But like all sugar highs, the crash was inevitable. Eventually, summer ended, the music faded, and we had to go back home—back to reality.

The carefree chaos of Berna's world stood in stark contrast to the future that awaited us on Long Hill—a house slowly unraveling, with parents who no longer fit together, and a childhood on the brink of change in ways we couldn't yet understand.

When I was eight years old, my mom and Snake separated because he had cheated on my mom with her best friend. He admitted to the affair. It was tense watching a family and relationships collapse.

My brother Mike and I would go to Snake's house for the obligatory overnight visits that were supposed to be routine, and uneventful.

Instead, Snake chose to repeatedly sexually abuse me. With just the two of us there—no mom to keep us safe, so no one to intervene—his vile behavior went unchecked.

I would fall asleep fast in my own bed and wake up somewhere else, confused, and disoriented. I realized that I was in Snake's bed in the middle of the night. A distinct feeling of wrongness settled over me as he hovered nearby, his presence heavy, and suffocating. There were signs that night and others, whispers of something off, something horrid, but I couldn't yet put words to the feeling—why it felt so icky, disgusting, and deeply, unnervingly wrong. I didn't know about sex—I was eight.

After the divorce, my mattress and my mom moved to another city. A couple of weeks later, while I was lying on my childhood bedroom floor, I woke to him naked next to my side. He had taken off my Strawberry Shortcake nightgown, and it was lying dead by my side. Strawberry Shortcake and Blueberry Muffin smiled back at me from Berry Bitty City, completely unaware of the evil unfolding at the base of Long Hill.

His violating touch prompted me to nervously ask, "What is happening right now?" He casually mentioned that he wanted to see "how much I had grown." As if he had a genuine interest in my growth—whether I'd gotten taller or lost a tooth. The answer was clearly rehearsed, but at that moment, we both knew the truth. He didn't care about me, my height, or my milestones. He cared only about himself, his perversion, and taking what was never rightfully his—my childhood: my innocence.

I retreated in sheer panic, my body seized with rigidity. An irreversible line had been crossed. I exiled myself to a faraway land, and left my body and emotions stashed away. I wanted to run away—Carrie's house or anywhere safe. But, at that exact moment, I instantaneously felt dirty, and unworthy of her friendship. My motionless body failed me. I was alone, with fear racing as an adult predator lurked beside me.

I asked to call my mom, and by the grace of God, he allowed it. The house I had grown up in, once filled with the comfort of familiarity—the TV by the kitchen, the bathroom across the hall, and the pictures lining the hallway—now felt foreign. Something had irrevocably altered the house and me—it had wiped clean the memories, erased like a bleached surface after a crime scene.

The phone dial tone rang in my ear as I waited for her to answer. At 1 am, it sliced through the silence like a blade. My mother answered on the second ring; her voice was thick with sleep but instinctively alert.

I sat on the edge of the couch, gripping the landline as if it were my only tether to solid ground. In the dimly lit corner of the living room, Snake perched on the old chair, its cushions worn thin by time and weight. His gaze was razor-sharp, dissecting every syllable that left my lips, searching for the slightest tremor of betrayal.

His dirty blonde bowl cut clung to his forehead in damp, uneven strands, a mess of sweat and neglect. He ran his fingers through it over and over—frantic, compulsive—like he could scrub away the filth, the sickness, the things that clung to him no matter how hard he tried to shake them off.

I kept my voice even, careful, monotone. Any crack or rise in pitch might set off alarms, and bring the situation crumbling down before I could act. "Mommy," I began, the childhood nickname slipping from my lips like a desperate plea for protection. "I can't sleep well. Can we meet at the park in the morning?"

Her voice softened instantly, the concern sharpening at the edges. "Of course we can. But is everything okay? Does your dad know you are calling?"

"Yes," I replied.

I hesitated, swallowing the knot that threatened to choke me. Snake shifted in the chair, with his knee bouncing in a nervous rhythm. His underwear-clad figure, so vulnerable yet menacing, felt like a grotesque parody of a man stripped of his façade. I forced myself to answer. "It's okay, but I just want to see you."

"Alright," she said, her voice laced with hesitation. "I'll see you in the morning."

The line clicked dead, and I let the receiver rest in its cradle. I didn't meet Snake's gaze as I muttered a hollow "goodnight" and trudged back to my room. Behind me, I could feel his tension radiating through the dim light; his thoughts were probably racing as fast as mine.

Back in my room, I climbed under the covers and pressed my head into the pillow, but sleep refused to come. My heartbeat reverberated in my ears, each thud a step closer towards the edge of the unfathomable. I closed my eyes and imagined that each pulse was the sound of a giant's footsteps, slow and methodical, growing louder with each beat. I told myself the giant was coming to carry me away, to scoop me up in its massive hands and transport me somewhere safe, somewhere far from this nightmare.

But the giant never came.

When the first light crept through the window, it felt cold and indifferent. There were no mystical creatures, no giants, and no heroes to carry me away from this reality. It was just me and the ticking clock, waiting for the next moment to unfold.

The bright colors of my Strawberry Shortcake dress clashed with the weight in my chest. The fabric brushed against my skin as I walked to the park, the familiar pattern, a fragile reminder of a childhood I wasn't sure I still belonged to. The swing set loomed ahead, its chains swaying faintly in the morning breeze. I climbed onto the seat; the metal was cold against my legs, as I began pushing myself back and forth, my feet scuffing the dirt with every swing.

I pushed the swing harder; the chains were groaning softly as my legs pumped nervously. My voice was small, trembling, but determined as I spoke.

In the morning light, with the innocence of childhood still clinging to me like the soft folds of my Strawberry Shortcake dress, all I knew was that the truth had to be spoken, no matter how much it hurt.

"Mommy, he touched me." My mom fell to her knees next to the park swing, unable to find an ounce of strength in the declaration. "I think it's happened before this, too." We swiftly moved off the swing and over to the police department where I confessed about the touching, and the signs, and received a crash course in the realities of abuse.

After this confession, our world crumbled.

Snake admitted his guilt and served a minimal sentence. It felt like someone had flipped the kitchen table of our lives—one violent upheaval that left everything shattered. The dishes were broken on the floor, but the real wreckage was harder to see: the sound of that breakage echoing in our ears, reverberating through our lives, unraveling everything we thought we knew.

My brother, my mom, and I spent years in purgatory—broke and broken.

We moved. Again, and again. Wandering like nomads with no stability, no roots, no sense of home.

We lost the magic of Christmas, the feeling of safety, the matching first-day-of-school outfits, the small comforts that made life feel normal.

Nothing was ever the same.

During my year of healing, I uncovered a painful truth—the abuse had gone on for years. That one night on Long Hill wasn't an isolated event; it was the final act in a long, silent violation.

While reading Gabor Maté's *The Myth of Normal*, a particular passage struck me. The wound I carried felt layered, built up over time like years of scar tissue, rather than the result of a single night in my bedroom. It was as if the abuse had been a scalpel, methodically severing my emotional body from my physical one—a disconnection born out of survival.

For the first time, I asked my mom a question she had never brought up, and one I had never thought to ask—until now.

"Mom, I was wondering... were there other signs before that night on Long Hill? Anything that made you question the abuse when I was younger? That this happened before I was eight years old?"

I recoiled as the words left my mouth, bracing for her response—for the weight of whatever truth might come next.

Then, with a reflective, quiet voice, she replied, "Actually, there were. When you were young, I took you to the pediatrician because you always had an unexplained, irritated vagina. I never thought to mention it and you never asked before."

When the pediatrician visits started, I was barely two years old. The enormity of that revelation meant that I had years of sexual trauma that had molded and shaped me into a lost little soul.

I don't know how, at just eight years old, I found the courage to speak the unspeakable. I understand why so many remain silent paralyzed by fear, by the absence of a safe harbor, by the unspoken rule that some truths are too dangerous to tell. But I also see the harshest truth of all: shame and denial, in their cruelest forms, do more than silence—they divide. They force families to choose sides, to turn their backs, and to pretend the wounds don't exist even as they bleed beneath the surface.

I learned this the hard way. The large extended family I had once known and loved treated me differently. Rumors swirled that Snake, and his family had connections with the judge, and that this was what secured him a minimal sentence of work release. In the aftermath, the three of us, my mother, my brother, and I—walked away from the only family we had ever known. We were no longer part of them; we were outsiders.

Someone had to bear the weight of his sins. He was someone's son, someone's brother, someone's blood. And in the end, the truth was too bitter a pill for Snake's family to swallow. Blaming a child—an adopted one at that—became the path of least resistance, the easiest sacrifice. I was the offering, the scapegoat, in their desperate attempt to protect their own.

The fallout from the abuse seeped into every corner of my being. Certain types of touch became perpetually uncomfortable. The family refused to acknowledge any truths spoken aloud. And the shame—like a parasite—took root, feeding off the silence.

By the time I was eight—maybe even earlier, I was already battling demons. The weight of that recognition crushed me, forcing my body to shut down, my mind to disconnect, and my emotional self to trail ten feet behind me, like a shadow I couldn't outrun.

I buried my broken soul six feet deep at the base of the Long Hill house, praying it would never claw its way back from the dead. But it lingered beneath the surface, festering. The years that followed were marked by relentless stomach aches, fueled by embers of shame. I carried an overwhelming hollowness, a slow decay that transformed me into something unrecognizable, a walking emotional zombie, alive in body but dead inside.

Years later, at 18, I found myself standing on Snake's front porch, the weight of the past pressing against my ribs. I needed answers. I needed justice.

I looked him in the eye and asked the question that had haunted me for a decade. He didn't flinch. He didn't waver. He simply denied it.

When I reminded him of his own confession, his response was chilling in its indifference.

"To save your eight-year-old reputation," he said.

There are moments in life when words fail, when people fail, or when the sheer cruelty of it all is so staggering that the air leaves your lungs. This was one of them.

The girl from Long Hill was forever changed that night. The moment she was molested, she left something behind—her innocence, her sense of safety, and her Strawberry Shortcake nightgown discarded on the bedroom floor. She no longer fit inside the soft world of childhood, where stories centered on baking and kindness. Magic ceased to exist.

Against her will, she stepped off the tracks of enchanted childhood—no Platform 9 ¾, no in-between. Just an abrupt arrival into a world she wasn't ready for. She walked away from eight years of life, with a part of herself buried so deep it would take decades to unearth it.

She developed a fear of men that clung to her well into her 30s. A simple touch—a hand grazing her back—sent a flinch through her body, an instinctive recoil that took years to unlearn.

She believed touch was dirty, though its meaning was more complicated than that, as it so often is for survivors.

That little girl became lost, wandering through a barren desert of humiliation, searching for something—anything—that felt like home.

And so, at 47, during my first ayahuasca journey, my intention was clear: I had to find her.

The first time I drank ayahuasca, terror gripped me—not just fear of the unknown, but fear that I might lose my mind entirely.

I wasn't just at rock bottom—I was beneath the barrel, buried in the damp darkness where the earthworms thrive.

Whether it was the weight of my life's circumstances or the sheer anticipation of what lay ahead, I had hit an all-time low.

Adding to the mess, I had broken a cardinal rule of preparing for an ayahuasca ceremony the night before—I had drunk alcohol. This is a major no-no. Now, sitting there with my nerves unraveling, I wasn't just questioning my life choices—I was questioning my readiness for what lay ahead.

Three consecutive nights of ayahuasca ceremonies stood between me and whatever came next. And as I sat there, with my stomach twisting, I couldn't help but wonder: Who would I be on the other side of this? Would my family recognize me? Would I even recognize myself?

Even after years of drinking beer, losing control—of my mind, my body, my reality—was something I had never been comfortable with. Control, in all circumstances, was my sanctuary—my shield.

At the start of the ayahuasca ceremony, the shaman asked everyone to set an intention. I played along, saying "healing" out loud for the group to hear. But inside, my intention was far less simple. I carried a secret mission, a massive to-do list written in the ink of old wounds. I wasn't here for just any healing—I was determined to accomplish a lifetime's worth of it in three nights.

I learned that plant medicine—and life—doesn't work that way.

When I entered the ceremony space, the shaman offered no warm greeting. His blue eyes met mine in a quiet acknowledgment—detached, and unreadable. It struck me as a missed opportunity, a moment where a simple gesture of comfort could have eased the weight of stepping into the unknown. So many arrive at this threshold, braving the psychedelic doorway with hearts full of fear and hope, longing for reassurance before the journey begins.

Broken hearts don't arrive alone; they bring battered souls, weary bodies, and frayed emotions with them. Often, they lack a solid spiritual foundation—adrift, uncertain, clinging to both nervousness and faith, hoping the psychedelic path might finally lead them home.

The lights dimmed, and the candles flickered as the shaman offered an opening prayer. Though the ceremony began at 10 pm, I arrived at 6 pm—ready, eager, and with too much time to think. As the hours dragged on, nervous energy tightened in my chest, mixing with exhaustion. By the time I drank my first cup of ayahuasca, my adrenal glands were spent, leaving me too drained to resist the bone-deep weariness settling in.

The medicine was thick and black, tasting of molasses and fermented prune juice, burning my empty stomach. After hours of fasting, the tar-like liquid churned inside me. There were no whispers of the journey ahead—only an overwhelming urge to vomit. I focused on slow, methodical breaths, willing the nausea to subside.

I felt scattered, as if I existed everywhere and nowhere at once. A part of me wondered if this disarray was just a distraction—because deep down, I feared the real work. I dreaded the cracking open, the emotional shell splitting apart, spilling everything raw and unguarded into the world.

Determined to keep my eyes open for at least an hour, I laid my head on the pillow—and failed, slipping to sleep almost instantly. When I woke—maybe an hour later—it felt like I had stepped into the wildest video game inside my head. Artificial cherries to collect, ghosts to devour—every flashing, chaotic element pulled straight from the Pac-Man games of my childhood.

I couldn't help but wonder what in the world this Amazonian brew was trying to teach me. The nonsensical video game playing in my mind made no sense. Frustration bubbled up—why was I wasting precious time when there was so much healing to do? My mind raced through an endless to-do list, with impatience creeping in. *I'm here to work, not play video games.*

But as I lay back and opened my eyes, I realized I couldn't change what was happening. Whether I understood it or not, this was part of the process. The only thing I could control was my response. And when I finally let go—the need to control, the resistance—I felt myself slowly opening up to the real work waiting beneath it all.

My eyes started silently leaking tears, slipping out like a quiet betrayal. It wasn't an active cry; there were no sobs or wailing, just a slow, steady release of something long pent-up. And it showed no signs of stopping.

I remember wanting to call my mom, or anyone who could anchor me in comfort. My nervousness about everything unfolding sat heavy in my chest, too much to process. Instead of facing it, I shut down. I passed out and fell asleep.

Over the course of the night and well into the next day, I cried. Tears streamed down my face, relentless, and uncontainable. By 11 am, I started to wonder if it would ever stop. It was cathartic but overwhelming—a flood of years' worth of trapped emotion breaking through the dam of my heart.

The tears finally slowed around 2 pm, when I joined a group in the open field for Qigong. As I stood there, still raw from the release, a large dog wandered over, giving me a once-over like he was assessing my emotional state. Then, without hesitation, he lifted his leg and tried to piss on me.

Somehow, that moment broke the spell. To this day, I've never been so grateful for an almost-urination situation. It was exactly the absurd, ridiculous reminder I needed that even in the heaviest moments, life still had a sense of humor.

On the second night of the ceremony, I got a full-blown mental ass-whooping—a no-excuses, get-off-the-couch-and-get-your-life-together kind of reckoning. The medicine wasn't gentle; it didn't whisper. It came at me hard, slamming down a fortified checklist of challenges. Healing—my original intention—was no longer a passive pursuit. It had been kicked into high gear, and I had no choice but to keep up.

Throughout the night, a voice kept barking, *'Let's get some shit done!'* At first, I wondered if ayahuasca had a potty mouth, only to realize it was my own voice, the same one I used to push myself in daily life. It was surreal to think that this revered plant medicine had morphed into a crass, no-nonsense drill sergeant, running a psychedelic boot camp in my mind. There were no breaks, and no mercy, just a relentless series of mental pushups.

For someone who had felt mentally unfit walking in, it was one of the most grueling missions I'd ever faced.

Once again, I approached the ceremony like it was my one shot at tackling the bulk of my trauma marathon crammed into a sprint at record-breaking speed. I wanted to get through it all because, truthfully, I wasn't sure I'd ever want to do this again.

By the end, I was bone-tired, but then alcohol surfaced as the next contender demanding my attention.

I questioned whether I wanted to keep drinking every night. Deep down, I already knew—I couldn't go back to sitting alone in my room, mindlessly watching TV with a drink in hand. Yet it would take months before I fully honored that truth. Ayahuasca made its stance on alcohol brutally clear, presenting it as the equivalent of a slow, nightly death.

Ceremony circles often describe alcohol as a low-vibration activity, but for me, it was more than that. With my history and the shadow of generational alcoholism, it wasn't just low, it was a zero, or maybe even a net-negative force in my life. The message was undeniable, even if it took time for me to listen to it.

Next, my mind drifted to Snake—to the destruction of my childhood. I saw myself at eight years old, reliving that terrible night at the base of Long Hill, a slideshow of moments that shattered my innocent worldview. I remembered the loss, and the way family members took sides after I told the truth at the police station.

Tears welled in my adult eyes, and I cried for that little girl.

I could feel my stepfather's denial, his shallowness, in every one of those moments. I saw his ego for what it truly was—fragile, twisted, built on lies. And I realized, with brutal clarity, how profoundly he had failed me—not just as a child, but as a baby. For years, maybe even still today, no one sees the danger he poses to his community. He's walked through life as if he's above me, weaving a narrative where I am the shameful one, the dirty one, while presenting himself as an upstanding member of society.

But during my ayahuasca journey, I saw the truth. The universe, the medicine, and God knew what had really happened. The damage, the deceit, and the weight of his choices: they lay squarely in his hands. The battle wasn't mine to fight anymore. It was between him and the Almighty. And somehow, knowing that brought me peace.

That night, I removed the welcome mat. The one that had silently read, *Snake, you're welcome to step on me, hold me down, and shame me. Come on in.* No more. He had no safe harbor in my body or my mind. He wasn't worthy—he was worth*less* to me.

With the help of ayahuasca, I envisioned extracting him from my body. Once he was out, I didn't know what to do with him. So, in my mind, I turned him into a loud, obnoxious rooster and set him loose on the streets of LA's Skid Row. Maybe, for once, he could serve a purpose—providing sustenance for the unhoused and hungry. But I figured his crowing at dawn would wear thin fast. Time wasn't on his side. Soon enough, a rotisserie BBQ would be in order.

I heard the call from the medicine giver—the offer of a second cup of ayahuasca. And I struggled. Deep down. I felt I had reached my limit for the night. My body screamed *no more!* But my mind, stubborn as ever, insisted: *You're here to heal. Keep going.*

The medicine giver told me I could have another cup if I could walk. So, against every signal my body sent, I forced myself forward. As I stepped up to receive the offer, tears streamed down my cheeks.

My eyes had once again betrayed me, purging in their own way. It wasn't sobbing, just an unrelenting release. It had been years since I had cried for myself, and now, I was making up for lost time.

The shaman whispered something into my cup, words that felt different from what he had spoken to the others. Then, he looked me in the eyes and said, *"Bless you."*

I drank. Within moments, my stomach lurched, and I started vomiting. Purging from ayahuasca comes in many forms—vomiting, crying, yawning, or everyone's favorite, diarrhea. My mind wanted to be tough, and to push through the pain, but I knew I had fulfilled my duty for the night. Relief washed over me.

I drifted in and out of an awakened state, spending most of the night facing the wall, my thoughts circling around one thing: concern for others. That's the warning they give at ayahuasca ceremonies— *this is an inside job.* And yet, for the first six months of participating, I couldn't shake it. Every cry, every wail, every whispered word in the dark pulled at me. I am a heart-driven, service-oriented person. Sitting still, and allowing others to suffer without stepping in, was its own kind of lesson—a hard one.

By the third night of the ceremony, I was bone-tired, drained of any will to unpack more emotional baggage. I slept through most of it. In ayahuasca circles, that's called "nada"—nothing.

For the first two nights, I felt completely out of place, like I didn't belong. But something shifted. At one point, I opened my eyes and saw people dancing in the center of the room, their movements alive with joy and connection. In that moment, an overwhelming sense of love and gratitude flooded through me—not just for them, but for all beings. Between bouts of sleep, I caught glimpses of pure magic—love unfolding, connection taking shape, a sense of belonging I hadn't felt before.

After the first night, I was ready to bolt, to get the hell out of Dodge. But what I learned is that no two nights are the same. Each one carries its own mystery, magic, or challenges its own invitation to heal. That third night, with its beautiful music, the dancing, and the sheer diversity of human experience surrounding me, gave me something unexpected: closure. If I had left, I would have missed the fullness of the experience and the transformation that comes from staying through discomfort.

At the final integration circle, something hit me—I had built my entire identity around my story. My past wasn't just a narrative; it was the lens through which I saw myself. And I was in for a rude awakening: my story wasn't just an obstacle, it was both my barrier to growth and, paradoxically, my path forward.

A common theme in journey work is the idea that we are made of stories. But how could I ever achieve a healthier mindset, when mine ran as deep as the Mariana Trench? My narrative was woven with themes of brokenness, shame, and the desperate lengths I had gone to in order to keep my secrets buried. My story wasn't just my truth, it was my armor, my prison, and the battle I had to face head-on.

The medicine giver had warned us before the ceremonies: *Don't come if you're stagnant. Don't come if you're watching violent movies, stuck in a habit loop, spending hours on social media, or eating a poor diet. It's bad for business.*

As he spoke, I felt like he was reading off my personal checklist. I could hear the click of each box being checked.

Stagnant? *Oh, absolutely—I've been parked here for years.*

Violent movies? *Of course!* Halloween *movies are practically a civic duty.*

Low-vibrational activities and social media? *That's my jam.*

And as for my poor diet? *Let's just say it's been a highly effective tool for shoving my emotions down, one slice of pizza at a time.*

Here's the thing: we all show up a little—or a lot—broken, often unaware that we've been living life at half-mast. And we don't realize it until we do.

I can't help but think that, if true self-awareness came easy, there would be a lot of financially broke shamans. Because really, *what's bad for business* seems to keep them *in* business.

Sometimes, we need a psychedelic jolt to shake us out of the toxic lull of our own existence. In that room, there were souls like mine—adrift, gasping for air, and desperate for a life raft in an ocean of despair. I grabbed hold as it pulled me to safety, though the safety was relative—a slow, uncertain drift through the Pacific, with the shore still impossibly far.

But then, in the distance, I saw a glimmer of dawn breaking through the clouds. A whisper of light: proof that maybe, just maybe, I might survive the year of healing.

"HOW"
Marcus Mumford (featuring Brandi Carlile)

CHAPTER 6

LEATHER, LIES AND A DIRTY COFFEE CUP

Chump strode into our lives with a cowboy hat perched on his head, wispy blonde hair, and a lanky frame stuffed into Wrangler jeans. He was, in every sense, a *mean-as-the-day-is-long* dickhead. His marriage to my mom took everyone by surprise. The reception was held in a random hotel banquet room in The Dalles, Oregon—an event that could only be described as *country bumpkin chic*. While the adults drank at the bar, we kids ran wild in a top-floor room, antagonizing the guests below. There wasn't a shred of elegance to be found.

It didn't take long for us to realize that, beneath his cowboy persona, Chump had *zero* redeeming qualities.

When I was about ten, my mom, my brother, and I moved to Redmond with Chump riding shotgun. He made custom prize saddles for the National Rodeo Finals, and though his craftsmanship was in high demand, his work ethic wasn't at the same level. The saddles were beautiful—when he *finally* finished them. Each one took months, or sometimes years, to complete.

Chump had originally started his career as a rodeo clown, but that dream had ended abruptly when a bull gored him in the back. The injury had left him jobless, bitter, and with a permanent hitch in his giddy up. The only thing more predictable than his complaints about his aching back was the steady stream of narcotics he used to numb them.

Chump opened a run-down saddle shop in the heart of Redmond—a place where the air hung thick with the scent of leather, oil, and wasted time. After school, my brother and I would race to the shop, stopping first at the grocery store across the street, where we were allowed to pick out a single piece of fruit as a snack.

Inside, Chump sat hunched over his workbench, sipping from a coffee cup that hadn't been washed in years—its contents a mystery best left unsolved. Scraps of leather were strewn across every plywood surface, a fitting reflection of his half-finished projects and the slow, meandering pace at which he worked. The shop was a world of its own, cluttered and grimy, a place where time stretched, and the smell of neglect clung to everything.

The bathroom, however, was the shop's true horror. Straight out of *Trainspotting*, it was a place where hovering was the only safe option, and touching anything was a risk not worth taking.

Visitors were rare, but one man—Ted—showed up like clockwork once a week. Balding and portly, he carried the easy charm of small-town gossip, always eager to share the latest news. He was a church scout leader, a title that should have signaled trustworthiness. But even at ten years old, I sensed something wasn't right.

The moment Ted walked in; a familiar dread crept over me. His presence was like a slow-moving shadow, something that felt off in a way I couldn't explain. The chime of the doorbell sent me retreating into the back of the shop, where my brother and I would huddle among scraps of leather and the remains of dead animals.

Every so often, Chump would leave Ted in charge while he ran errands. At the time, it seemed harmless enough. But looking back, I knew better—my unease wasn't just a child's imagination. It was a warning. Something about Ted was deeply, undeniably wrong.

Suffering was inflicted upon me at the hands of evil men, sharpening my intuition against danger like a blade. My instincts had never led me astray, and Ted was no exception. I later heard the story of Lou, a scout who had suffered years of sexual abuse, before reporting it. After pleading guilty at the hearing, a judge ordered Ted to serve 20 days in jail and three years of probation. Both the scouts and the church had failed to sound the alarm, giving Ted the time he needed to inflict harm on at least 15 young boys over 28 years.

When Lou was 17 years old, he served his form of justice, killing Ted with a sawn-off shotgun at close range to ensure that he would no longer harm children. But not all monsters are exposed with such a newsworthy scandal. Some wear masks, hiding in plain sight, deceiving those closest to them.

It was clear that Chump was one of the greatest actors the world had ever seen. When my mom was around, he played the role of the sweet, attentive father figure with unsettling ease—serving us dinner, making small talk about our day, feigning the warmth of a man who belonged in a family. For those moments, he almost passed as normal.

But the second the door closed behind my mom as she left for work, the mask slipped. In an instant, he became someone else—a cruel, seething presence who thrived on control and fear. His words cut like knives, his hands weren't always idle, and his temper ruled the house. My brother and I lived in the grip of a walking contradiction, the embodiment of Jekyll and Hyde.

I was around 11, and Mike was 8, when we learned the art of vigilance—always on guard while our mom worked long hours. We moved through the house like shadows, careful, quiet, trying to stay out of Chump's line of sight.

Even so, Mike carried an almost reckless sense of lightness, as if the weight of our reality never quite settled on his shoulders. With his dirty blonde hair and gap-toothed grin, he was caught in that fleeting space between boyhood and manhood, radiating humor and mischief. While fear and caution consumed me, Mike seemed untouched by the darkness that surrounded us—he was either oblivious to it or willfully refusing to let it take place. His head remained planted firmly in the sand of denial, a stubborn defiance against a world that had already demanded too much from us.

We kept the truth from my mom for as long as we could, our silence rooted in both fear and protection. Chump's abuse had instilled terror so scary that speaking up felt like a gamble with our own survival. But beyond that, we couldn't bear to add to my mom's burden. She worked relentlessly, coming home each night bone-tired, worn down from the sheer effort of keeping our family afloat. Watching her push through exhaustion was painful enough—it didn't feel right to pile on weight.

One weekend, while my mom was away on a trip, Chump was kind to me. The shift was so jarring, so out of character, that it felt like I was being courted. I was 13 years old, and I knew better than to believe in his sudden change in tone. That night, I slept behind my bedroom door for added security, every muscle in my body tense, waiting. I heard pacing outside my door—it felt predatory. His kindness wasn't kindness at all—it was calculated, another weapon in his arsenal of control. His cruelty was predictable, but this? This was something far more insidious. I never let my guard down. Not ever.

During our time in Redmond, we moved houses twice. Even when we settled in one town, we felt like we lived in the perpetual state of U-Haul. Despite the transitory nature of my life, I had two friends, Jenny and Kate. Jenny and her sister Kira were raised by their mother Norna, who was relatively normal and ran a daycare from home. Jenny and Kira had a taste for nice things, which always left me feeling envious. When Esprit and Benetton were all the rage, I longed for their fashionable clothes.

I saved up all my money to buy a grape-colored button-up Benetton shirt, which became my pride and joy. Since we were in a lower income bracket, I often found myself in a constant state of envy, bad haircuts, and four long years of braces. Life felt unfair but I was always grateful to visit Jenny's house, where good snacks and a sense of normalcy were always in abundance.

Kate came from a suitable home, with a mother who adored her and a stepfather who loved her just as much. She had the blondest hair, a sweet nature, and seemed to be well-adjusted. Visiting her house felt like stepping into country life, as she lived on the outskirts of town. We spent our time throwing rocks at each other from safe distances, running around the expansive fields, and sitting in front of the TV when we grew tired of our shenanigans.

About a year into our friendship, Kate told me something in the most sacred of confidences—sealed with a double pinky swear. The secret was that her 18-year-old step brother was sexually violating her in a horrific way. I entrusted my own mother with that terrible secret, one too heavy for my small shoulders to bear alone. I made her promise to keep it, believing that, if she held it too, maybe it wouldn't feel so suffocating.

Some secrets, even sealed with pinky swears, should never remain hidden. But betrayal has a sound—a hushed voice, a careful pause, the weight of words never meant to be shared.

One Saturday afternoon, with my ear pressed against my bedroom door, I heard it. My mother, divulging the truth to Kate's mother.

The ripple effect was immediate. A shift in the air, a sense of something slipping from my grasp. Some wounds come from the hands of strangers, but others—*the worst ones*—come from the people we trust to keep us safe. I struggled with the betrayal of a friend's secret, coupled with the reality that I had ensured that the abuse would stop. She was safe, but it cost me a friendship.

Kate's father went home, beat the shit out of his son, and kicked him out of the house.

That marked the end of my friendship with Kate. Our once-strong bond had become too strained to repair. Sometimes I wonder if broken or lost souls naturally gravitate toward each other, like magnets. We understand each other in ways most people can't fathom—especially when we're clawing our way out of a muddy grave.

I wonder if the scout leader, Ted, had further-reaching consequences than I ever realized. Kate's brother, a former scout, was the same age as the man who shot Ted. The questions linger and the answers remain elusive.

We moved to Boulder City, Nevada, where Chump worked out of the attached garage. This brought a new level of difficulty. With no shop to go to, Chump was home with us full-time—an inescapable, toxic presence. Moving the saddle shop to our garage made Chump a constant presence in our lives. It felt like living with black mold that seeped into every part of the house, but it was Chump—always in his tight Wranglers and pearl-buttoned shirts.

Weekends were the worst. My mom and Chump would lock themselves in their bedroom, and we would sit outside, waiting for hours just to spend a few moments with her. Despite her hard work, he stole those weekends, our only chance to be with her.

Chump maintained strict control over food, chores, and communication in our household. Each month, I had the unenviable task of finding and killing the black widows under the kitchen sink, vacuuming the house, ironing his underwear, and completing a random assortment of other chores. These responsibilities ensured he could spend his days chain-smoking in front of the TV, only appearing productive when my mom returned.

Food, especially Oreos, was another means of control. Chump hoarded sweets, saying that they were off-limits. He would threaten us with serious consequences if we so much as touched them. Every week, in quiet defiance, I would steal two cookies, analyzing the rows to ensure my theft went undetected. Years of sneaking food from an oppressor more recently made me wonder if my habit of overstocking my freezer in adulthood stemmed from a learned survival instinct or growing up poor.

We had a dog, Brandy, who bore the brunt of Chump's unpredictable temper. If the mood struck, he'd drop-kick her across the room—yet somehow, she remained *his* dog. I suppose, like the rest of us, she knew there was no escaping the fact that Chump was the Alpha.

Chump drove an old Dodge van—the kind that looked like it belonged in the grainy reenactments of every after-school special, warning kids about stranger danger. Inside, faded orange shag carpet clung to every surface, trapping the thick stench of cigarette smoke and stale upholstery.

His business logo was slapped across the side, an unintentional punchline that quickly became a running joke among my friends. *Chump Dump Saddles*, earned him the nickname "Dump Chump." But the laughter wasn't just about the sign—my friends had their own stories about him. Chump didn't limit his cruelty to the privacy of our home. He made sure there was an audience of my peers.

Whenever I stayed with my grandparents in Oregon, and the Greyhound schedule didn't line up, Chump was the one who had to come and get me. That meant two long days trapped in the van, crawling across the Nevada desert with no air conditioning and nothing but the suffocating heat and Chump's cigarette smoke filling the space between us. The endless stretch of sun-scorched highway, with either oppressive silence or the constant hum of his voice spewing complaints out into the void—these trips were a personal version of hell.

Riding beside the self-proclaimed King of Shit Mountain, I'd press my face into that disgusting shag carpet just to escape the cloud of smoke. It was misery in its purest form, worse than any Greyhound bus ride could ever have been.

The daily stress of our home life weighed on my brother Mike even sooner than it did on me. He started lighting fires—not out of mischief, but as a desperate attempt to externalize the chaos burning inside him. It put him in the spotlight, but not in the way he needed. Instead of help, he got punished.

One of my first memories of living with Chump was the gutwrenching helplessness of trying to protect my brother and failing at every turn. I remember Mike being tossed around the living room like a rag doll over something as insignificant as a missed homework assignment. He endured regular beatings for nothing more than being a child, each blow a cruel reminder that, in Chump's world, we were powerless.

A business owner I knew once mentioned they would address physical and sexual abuse in the workplace, but verbal abuse seemed like a lesser concern—a background noise to more tangible harms. It made me wonder, *does verbal abuse count?*

Over the years, through countless conversations, I've noticed a perception that verbal abuse is something you can just muscle through with a little mental toughness, an outlier to the *more serious* physical abuses. But in my experience, that couldn't be further from the truth. Words don't fade; they etch themselves into the psyche, shaping self-worth, altering reality, and leaving scars that no one else can see.

Bruises fade. Words burrow. They settle deep inside you, growing roots, tangling into your sense of self until you can't tell where the insult ends and where you begin. Words are scars that don't show on the skin but run just as deep. They live in the way a person hesitates before speaking, the way they brace for hurt even when none is coming, and the way they shrink themselves to fit into a world that once made them feel small.

Chump never had to lift a hand to break me. He did it with a word, a glance, or a well-placed insult that lodged itself in my psyche like shrapnel.

"Slut."

"Worthless."

"Idiot."

I was none of those things, but when I heard them enough, I didn't just believe them—I became them. Not because they were true, but because fighting it felt impossible. My mind adapted to survival, even when that meant accepting Chump's lies as my own reality.

It took decades to strip those words away—to remind myself that the things Chump said reflected *his* sickness, *his* emptiness, not mine.

The horrible names clung to my skin, sank into my clothes and became the air that I breathed. In the malleability of my youth, the words transformed into a jaded north star—broke me, split me open, and exposed an evil I never imagined could become the force guiding me through life. Verbal abuse wasn't something I could "muscle through"—it was a poison that reshaped my core.

Before the full weight of those words settled in, I was convinced I was destined for the clergy of some unknown church. I don't recall exactly where I found God or how my fierce belief in the Bible took root, but in hindsight, I imagine it was born out of sheer desperation. Determined to become a nun, I spent my free time praying and preaching. My friends couldn't utter a bad word without receiving a stern lecture, and using the Lord's name in vain? That was a direct invitation for me to recite Bible passages, urging them to repent.

With braces, headgear, and a determination to preach the glory of God, I found myself relegated to the teenage sidelines. I kept friends during this self-righteous, silver-tongued phase—a fact that remains one of the biggest mysteries of my life.

Looking back, I see now that my connection to God was a desperate attempt to save not just myself, but my family. Each day, I would strap on the God armor, preparing myself for battle against dark forces. Chump was the embodiment of darkness.

During that time, I had two saviors who kept sanity and humor parked right on my doorstep. One of them was Marla, who came from a large Mormon Māori family that had moved to Boulder City,

Nevada, straight from New Zealand. She had four siblings, each with a personality so distinct that their house was a prime spot for people-watching.

Marla's mom was a petite woman with a refined accent and a permanent air of frazzled exhaustion, as if life had been running just a step ahead of her for years. She bleached her hair blonde and wore heavy makeup, her beauty routine an elaborate production we never tired of watching.

In about five minutes flat, she could empty an entire can of Aqua Net—I'm convinced she must have owned stock in the company. As she meticulously applied her makeup, Marla and I sat nearby, throwing out snarky suggestions, like whether borrowing one of her husband's paintbrushes might speed up the process. She'd swat at us like flies, adding us to the ever-growing list of daily nuisances that came with raising five kids.

I often hung out at Marla's house, even when she wasn't there, it was my escape from the realities of home. The chaos in her household was so entertaining I'd sit in the living room with a bag of popcorn, waiting for the daily comedy show to begin.

Marla's father was a traditional Māori man—dark-skinned, thick-accented, and exuding a serious air that didn't quite match the family's otherwise chaotic energy. A painter by trade, he drove what had to be the longest station wagon known to man. He'd drop us off at school, but as teenagers, we'd make him stop at least a block away from the entrance. We'd slink out with our backpacks, hoping to go unnoticed, as paint supplies inevitably tumbled out alongside us. And just when we thought we'd made a clean getaway, he'd drive by with a honk and a wave, keeping us humble.

Marla's sister—Party Patricia, or PP, as we affectionately called her, was a legendary pleasure-seeker and an honorary mayor of the local party scene. At least once a week, she'd vanish into the night (or sometimes into the next afternoon), triggering Marla's mom to sound the alarm. With her crisp accent and no-nonsense urgency, she'd rally the troops and pile us into one of their family's three prized Pontiac Fieros—because why own one when you can have a fleet? Braces gleaming, binoculars in hand, and seat belts… Well, they were optional unless we doubled up. But if fate cursed us with the station wagon for the retrieval mission, we all paid the price, especially Patricia, whose grand return was dampened by the sheer social horror of rolling up in a bona fide jalopy.

The ensuing hunt was always ridiculously hilarious. We'd scour the house of every guy aged 16 to 20 in the area, searching for PP and her latest male "perp." I took great pride in my role as the official door knocker, and with my unwavering faith in the Almighty, it only seemed right that I should lead the noble charge—righteous in purpose, determined in execution, and utterly convinced we were carrying out a divine mission.

At 14 years old, I'd knock with authority, ask if they'd seen the elusive Patricia, and—without fail—the guy would shake his head and say, "Nope, haven't seen her." We all knew better. She was holed up inside, probably rolling her eyes at our amateur detective work.

On the rare occasion when Patricia needed a ride home, we considered it a hard-won victory. But about 90% of the time, we came up empty-handed. Not that it mattered. The real prize wasn't finding her—it was the thrill of the Boulder City chase.

Marla had been raised in a devout Mormon family, though most of her siblings drifted away from church service as they reached young adulthood. Her father, however, remained steadfast in his faith, carrying the spiritual torch for the entire family.

Somehow, Marla and I ended up befriending Sister J, a Mormon woman from the neighborhood who, despite her devotion, had the lively energy of someone constantly teetering on the edge of chaos. With the frazzled look of a strung-out homemaker, she was an unexpected addition to our duo. To this day, we still have no idea how this unlikely trio came to be.

Some afternoons after school, Marla and I would head to Sister J's house for snacks, lively soap opera commentary, and trampoline jumping. When we'd had our fill of those activities, we'd convince Sister J to take us on a drive around Boulder City to scope out the local scene. She always obliged, leaving her kids behind without a second thought.

I believe that Sister J saw us as her equal, especially when we swapped unfiltered opinions on *Days of Our Lives*. And trust me, we had *plenty* to say about the heartache, deception, and tangled love affairs that kept that show running.

Then there was Allen, one of my best friends growing up. He was nearly six feet tall, with curly brown hair and a frame so thin it seemed a strong gust of wind could take him out. His parents were the epitome of normal—his dad, a teacher and football coach, his mom, a chiropractic assistant. Their house was immaculate, the kind of place where shoes were left by the door, and something was always baking in the oven, filling the air with the comforting scent of home.

It had all the makings of a Norman Rockwell painting—except for one thing: Allen's sister, Britt, was a certified loose cannon.

Britt got into hard drugs early and had a baby in high school. We were all worried when Allen told us the baby's lollipop had been lying on the meth plate. Despite the whirlwind of chaos surrounding Britt, Allen's home was a refuge for me—a place where normality, humor, and friendship kept us anchored in a world that often felt anything but steady.

Allen and I had a routine of meeting halfway between our houses in the Boulder City Cemetery. As we walked back together, I insisted we stop at each grave and say, *"I'm sorry."* I'm not sure why I felt compelled to make Allen participate in this ritual, but he never questioned it—he just went along with it.

Even now, whenever I pass a cemetery, I still take a moment to acknowledge those who have passed. It's my way of saying, *"I see you, thank you, and now, if possible, I'd like safe passage."*

Allen and I shared a bond that went deeper than most friendships at that age. We were just two teenagers, but there was an unspoken understanding between us—one I clung to. I spent countless hours with him, confiding in ways I couldn't with anyone else. He listened without judgment, got angry on my behalf, and, when I didn't have the strength to stand up for myself, he did it for me.

One day, as we walked into the house, Chump looked me in the eye and called me a *slut*—right in front of Allen. Without hesitation, Allen—who barely weighed 110 pounds—stepped between us and told Chump to knock it off. The room went silent as they locked eyes, with the tension thick in the air. Allen didn't flinch. He didn't back down. He stood his ground against a man twice his size because, for that moment, my dignity mattered more than his fear.

That act cemented him in my heart forever. It was a small act of defiance, but to me, it was everything. In a world where I often felt powerless, Allen reminded me that I wasn't invisible—and that I was worth defending.

Chump's insults were as predictable as they were cruel: always *idiot, worthless* and his favorite, *slut*. The irony was almost laughable.

I was a virgin who praised God, read the Bible, and clung to my faith like a lifeline, yet he wielded that word like a weapon, trying to break me with it.

I was the kind of person who befriended both boys and girls, never thinking twice about it. But to Chump, that was all the evidence he needed to brand me with his judgment. It didn't matter who I was, only the version of me he wanted to tear down.

The real kicker came the day Marla, and I stumbled upon an entire box of VCR porn tapes hidden in the house. There were so many that disgust didn't even begin to cover it—the sheer volume left us speechless. It was obvious who was really engaging in *slutty* behavior behind closed doors. I couldn't help but wonder if Chump's secret stash was the real reason his customers' custom saddles took so damn long. Even then, I saw the hypocrisy for what it was.

Maybe it happened all at once, or maybe it was over the slow, grinding passage of years—but at some point, the abuse shattered me. I stopped caring: about school, about myself, and about anything. I walked through the world feeling exposed, certain that everyone could see the monster that lived in my home and, with that, came judgment. Some took advantage of the vacancy in my eyes, the way I carried my hollowed-out self. And I don't even blame them, I was easy prey.

Chump was the butt of every joke in my friend's group, and we did our best to laugh through the darkness. But there was nothing funny about what was waiting for me at home. I stopped caring how I dressed, my grades slipped, and I let myself sink into the abyss. And through it all, God was silent. No matter how hard I prayed, no matter how desperately I reached for something, I could not hear, sense, or feel the presence I had once believed in. The heavens had shut me out. I was alone.

I started drinking, running with a wild skateboarding crew of mis-fits with too much freedom and nowhere to place our anger. Most of us had single mothers who worked long hours, leaving us to roam, push boundaries, and test the limits of recklessness.

It was in the grimy house of the skateboarding ringleader that I had sex for the first time—on a sheetless waterbed, in a room that reeked of stale beer and bad decisions. There was no love, no tender-ness, and no meaning. Just another act of detachment, another way to sever myself from the girl I had once been. I had spent so long being hurt that I wanted to hurt others in return—anyone within reach, but most of all, myself.

The saying "hurt people, hurt people" rang painfully true—I had turned that hurt inward, wounding myself in ways both seen and unseen. I became unrecognizable. The girl who had once cared about grades, about her future, and about right and wrong—she was gone. I cast aside the Bible, along with the version of myself who had clung to it so desperately, leaving them both behind in the trash.

As my grades slipped, I got a 'C' on my report card. And I knew that meant that Chump would make me pay. In desperation, I asked some older teenagers to "fix" it; in the end, there was a chunk of paper removed from the grade slip—the paper was beyond repair. And that meant I was in bigger trouble.

I left the report card on the table, walked to the bathroom cabinet and downed whatever pills I could find. I lay quietly on my bed with my arms folded across my chest, waiting patiently to die. I wrote a goodbye letter to my mother, poured out every ounce of love I had for her. I wanted her to know that none of this was her fault, that I had always loved her, and was sorry for getting a 'C.'

Chump walked in, read the note, looked at me lying there, and then—without a word—walked right back out the door. As far as he was concerned, if I took myself out, that was one less problem for him. I lay there for hours, dizzy, with my stomach twisting, waiting for the inevitable. But death never came. I don't even remember what I took, only that I felt sick and disoriented, hovering somewhere between despair and survival. Whether I believed in God or not, one thing was clear—it was not my time to go.

Hours later, my mom came home. Chump, with all the ease of a habitual liar, told her the neighbors had asked me to babysit, so he had sent me on my way. He mentioned to my mom about the report card and that I was grounded for a month. And just like that, the truth of that day vanished. My mother never knew. To her, it was just another ordinary day. And Chump? He didn't care. Neither did I.

Eventually, Mike made the only choice that offered him a way out—he left. He chose to live with his biological father, a man who had molested me for years. It was a decision born out of sheer survival, a lesser evil in a world where no option was truly safe. That completely shattered us all.

It was no longer the three dirt-poor amigos under one roof in the sweltering Nevada sun. After Mike left, it felt like my mom and I were walking through life on broken glass, each step a reminder of a painful loss.

He stole my only brother from me, ripping away the one person who truly understood our shared reality. With that loss came a deep sense of betrayal. I understood why Mike had needed to leave—I even knew it was the only way he could escape—but that didn't stop me from feeling abandoned.

Once he fell into Snake's clutches, it was no longer my brother's choice. It became a battle dictated by the legal system; one we were too poor to fight. Money determined justice, and we had none.

My brother was gone, and there wasn't a single human capable of pulling him back.

His options were living with a sexual molester or a physical and psychological abuser. No one can sit in judgment of that choice— but in my teenage ignorance, I did. I let my sadness at Mike's departure twist itself into anger, unfair and misplaced. It was easier to be mad than to admit how deeply I missed him, or how lost I felt without him.

I don't carry many regrets, but if I could rewrite those years, I would have been softer with him. I would have told him the truth— not just about my pain, but also about how much I understood him. I wish I had embraced his decision with the shattered-hearted love that we both deserved.

Not long after my brother moved out, the spotlight had nowhere left to turn but onto me. I could no longer slink through the shadows unnoticed—I was the last one standing, the only person left in the house with Chump from dusk till dawn. His moods swung wildly, his chain-smoking left a constant haze in the air, and when he wasn't glued to the TV, he was out in the garage, *pretending* to work on saddles. The rest of the time, he hurled insults like a crazed monkey, daring me to fight back, or to challenge him.

The day Mike left, the house became quieter, more shadowy, and yet somehow heavier. I should have felt relief for him having found a way out. Instead, I felt like a soldier abandoned on the battlefield, left to fend for myself under Chump's reign.

In the silence of his absence, I wondered: *Was he wrong to go? Is there ever a way out for me too?*

The weight of that loss settled into my bones, but instead of grieving, I did what I had always done—survived. I moved through the days like a ghost, tiptoeing around Chump's moods, watching the door, and waiting for Mike to walk back in. But he never did.

For years, I told myself I was angry at my brother for leaving. The truth? I was angry at the world for making us choose between two evils. I was angry that I never got a choice.

One morning, I told Chump I'd be hanging out with friends after school—Allen, Marla, and our friend Jennifer. That afternoon, we walked into the house to drop off my backpack, stepping into a thick cloud of cigarette smoke, with the stale air clinging to our clothes. I reminded Chump of my plans, but he immediately shut me down. He *needed* me to stay and wait for the UPS driver, he said—he had an errand to run. His tone made it clear this wasn't a request.

I pushed back. It was a simple request—an afternoon with friends. But Chump never needed much of an excuse. The argument escalated in seconds, and before I knew it, he had his hands on me.

In front of my friends, he grabbed me by the throat, lifted me off my feet, and pressed me against the living room wall. The room blurred at the edges, not just from lack of air but from the sheer disbelief that this was happening—with an audience. Chump had made sure of that. He wanted them to see.

Allen tried to intervene, but none of us really knew what to do. We were just kids, frozen in place as the weight of what had just happened settled in. I stayed home that night, hiding in my bedroom—humiliated, terrified, and trapped.

Jennifer, who came from a kind Mormon family, told her parents. Her father called my mom and offered me a place to stay. That call was a lifeline. I didn't end up moving in with them, but a few months later, my mom made a decision that would change everything: she took a job on a tiny island called Saipan in the South Pacific. And just like that, we were gone.

I remember boarding the plane, leaving behind the familiar desert landscape for an island chain that felt hidden in the middle of nowhere. But what we didn't know as we flew toward our new life was that back home, Chump's secrets were unraveling.

Back in Nevada, Chump had taken a trip to Oregon and flown back home. Without him knowing my mom had asked my aunt to pick him up from the airport. She arrived early—just in time to watch him run straight into the arms of another woman.

Years later, I would learn the final, twisted truth—my junior high friend's older brothers had been selling Chump cocaine. For years, we had been living under the same roof with a chain-smoking, cheating, abusive coke addict. The town knew. The whispers had been there all along.

The secret was out.

Chump left wreckage in his wake. For me, it was a fall from grace. I no longer believed in God. After everything I had endured, it felt like He had failed me. The relationship fractured beyond repair—my balled-up fists raised to the sky, demanded answers. That moment mirrored my own reckoning. I had lost faith, not just in God, but in life itself.

Over time, God and I called a truce, but walked in different directions. It was never the same again.

Perhaps that's why, when I finally committed to a year of healing through therapeutic psychedelic sessions, I had to face it all—Chump's wreckage, the loss of my brother, my innocence, and even God.

Six months into my year of healing, I took part in a three-night ayahuasca ceremony. On the second night, the figure returned—no longer a distant presence but fully formed, stepping out from the shadows. It was the same one I'd first encountered in the garden, during that gentle psilocybin journey meant only to dip my toes in. Back then, it had stayed at the edges. But now, it stood before me.

A voice, calm and deliberate, echoed in my mind: "Do you remember the dark figure that day in the garden?"

I did.

It had been waiting—not to frighten me, but to be seen.

"Yes," I answered, with the memory still vivid.

The voice replied, "That's you—all the darkness, trauma, and pain from your childhood abuse. You carry it with you wherever you go. It's heavy and weighing you down. Would you like to let it go?"

Without hesitation, I answered: "Yes. I'm more than ready."

That night, lying on a mat as the sounds of purging echoed around the room, I experienced one of the most profound healings of my life. It felt as if layers of darkness were being stripped from my body, one block at a time. I cried, yawned, and vomited, releasing years of trauma that had consumed me. It was relentless, deep work, as though my body and spirit finally unburdened themselves after carrying the weight for so long.

By the end of the night, I was certain I had purged everything—that I was completely healed. But the medicine had other plans. Life lessons are rarely that simple.

Feeling lighter than I had in years, I stepped into the final night of the ceremony, convinced my healing was complete. I drank the ayahuasca, set my intention, and settled in. But just as I began to surrender, a voice cut through the stillness—clear, unmistakable.

"Katie, you forgot about shame."

In an instant, fear and shame crashed over me, two relentless forces that had shaped me, haunted me, and dictated far too much of my life. Their weight returned like an old, unwelcome companion—a raw, visceral reminder of the vulnerability that had left me exposed to toxic behaviors, destructive people, and the heaviness of emotions I thought I had escaped.

I realized there had been people in my life who had rifled through my emotional drawers, leaving them empty. In response, I had become the architect of my humiliation, choosing a path of overconsumption, numbness, and poor decisions. Initially, others inflicted shame, but eventually, I took over the job myself.

I had gone from the confidence of standing on a metaphorical pulpit, declaring my healing, to the sobering realization that it's far more complicated. Healing isn't a one-time proclamation; it's a continuous, often messy process. I had underestimated just how deeply shame's roots still ran through me.

For years, I carried my past like a second skin, heavy and unrelenting. Even when I thought I had let go, it clung to me—whispering reminders, dragging me backward.

But that night, as I stood face-to-face with the darkness, I understood something I never had before: *it was once mine, but it no longer had to be.*

I hadn't just survived Chump. I hadn't just survived the childhood that tried to break me.

I woke up.

His words, his cruelty, his presence, they no longer defined me. They were not worthy of being the sum of my story.

I claimed my life back.

I stayed in the arena. I faced the demons. And I walked out victoriously.

Pulling out those rotted roots was an exorcism of everything I had once believed would define me. It was painful, deliberate, and divine. And when the last of them was gone, I stood in the wreckage and realized *I was never alone.*

God had been waiting, patient as ever, for me to return. Through grace, we found each other again—not as we had once been, but as we were always meant to be.

"WE DON'T EAT"
James Vincent McMorrow

CHAPTER 7

TOO FRACTURED TO CATCH THE FALL

R unaways always seemed to cause problems in my social circles, but this incident was a new level of absurdity. It left me wondering how my life had spiraled into such chaotic territory.

Allen, my best friend from Nevada, was one of those runaways—the kind who called last-minute from the road, already halfway across a state line. "Hey Katie, I'm on my way to Boise. Can I crash for a while?"

By then, I had become the unofficial runaway refuge for lost kids from Boulder City. They always found me, no matter where I moved—something about my life orbiting enough chaos to make their own feel safe. I had a network of friends running full-time party houses, so I could usually offer a couch, a floor, or at least a warm burrito.

Allen showed up barefoot, behind the wheel of a borrowed car. We walked into a fast-food joint like everything was normal. I looked down and asked, "Hey Allen, great to see you. Got shoes?"

"Nope," he said nonchalantly. "I was in a hurry to leave—didn't bring them."

It was...complicated. Allen's parents were as ideal as they came, so his MacGyver getaway in a Volvo station wagon didn't make much sense to me. I think he just wanted to give running away a try, to see how it would pan out—a teenage rite of passage, another notch on the *been there, done that* belt.

At the end of my junior year of high school, I went to visit Allen in Las Vegas. During my visit, his parents made an unexpected request— they asked me to move in with them to help Allen get through his final year of school.

By then, I had perfected the art of appearing *normal* to the outside world. I'd convinced people I was a well-adjusted, responsible teenager. Childhood had equipped me with a variety of tools I could use to play convincingly, get decent grades, have good hygiene, and manage to hold thoughtful conversations with adults. On the surface, I seemed like I had it all together. But it was just an act, a carefully crafted performance to stay under the radar.

When Allen's parents sat me down at the kitchen table while he was out running an errand, they shared their concerns. Allen was struggling with drugs and alcohol, and they were at a loss—desperate to help him, unsure of how to reach him. They believed my presence might make a difference and offered me the chance to finish my senior year living in their home.

To me, it felt like another wild detour—a chance to escape, reconnect with old friends, and maybe pretend things weren't as messy as they were. So I said yes.

The only person fully aware that I was in no position to "help" Allen with his cocktail of dysfunctions? That would've been me. I was knee-deep in my own reckless behavior, just better at dressing it up. I wore my chaos well—high-functioning, polite, and clean enough to pass as a solution.

Although Allen and I had stayed in touch over the years as I moved from Saipan to Boise, we hadn't lived in the same town for what felt like a lifetime. Teenage years and dog years seemed to work the same, where each year felt like seven in my life. I knew Allen still loved me as more than a friend, but I couldn't bring myself to love him in the same way as I had.

I was broken—deeply so—and in a phase of breaking things around me. I typically shattered relationships or attempted to break myself. But Allen was different. He was something I was simply unwilling to break. I owed him that much for all the sacrifices he had made, especially with Chump. I loved him deeply, but not in the way he needed or deserved. And because I was so fractured, I couldn't allow him to become a part of my broken process.

When I moved in during my senior year, I had a blast reconnecting with old friends, but I never dated Allen. That choice, though necessary, broke both of our hearts in ways neither of us fully understood at the time.

Years earlier, when Allen would walk me home from school, I'd pour my anger into our conversations, trying to articulate what it felt like to open the door to my house and step into suffocating darkness. As I waved goodbye to his compassionate presence, I returned to a home where light was shut out—both literally and figuratively.

He came from a good home, with parents who loved him. His house smelled of fresh cookies, and grandparents stopped by unannounced to share laughter and warmth. I suppose it was hard for him to comprehend the gravity of a home that felt the complete opposite.

Mine reeked of stale cigarettes, with blinds drawn tight to ensure no light ever seeped in.

I felt damaged, and my brokenness kept me from embracing Allen's purity and unwavering love. Years would pass before I reached my own moment of reckoning. Until then, I carried the belief that I was unworthy of love.

That reckoning came with a primal scream—a day of crying and rage pouring out of me, seeping into the sheets beneath me. *How dare Chump damage us in all the ways that he did.* The storm unearthed years of boiling inner turmoil, and when it finally subsided, it left behind a glimmer of something unexpected: a small respite.

Allen had been my protector, but I realized that to truly heal, I had to confront the weight of the past on my own. I needed to find my moment of reckoning, to release the pain, even if that release felt incomplete or fleeting. It took me years to finally direct my anger and grief at the people and places that had buried the dark secrets in their carefully crafted façades.

I never got the chance to properly thank Allen before he passed in his mid-40s from years of pill-popping and excessive alcohol consumption. I was never able to fulfill his or his parent's wishes.

I moved out of Allen's house halfway through my senior year, once it became clear to him—and his family—that I wouldn't date him or be the solution to his sobriety. Looking back, I realize now that I wasn't even in the right frame of mind to save myself, let alone someone else.

Allen's parents' belief that I could somehow save him felt ludicrous at the time, but in hindsight, I can see why they might have thought so. I had always projected an image of cool composure—I seemed collected, controlled, and unshakable. They mistook that exterior for the kind of strength capable of offering the steady, open-hearted presence their son needed—but I had spent my whole life bracing for impact, not softening into connection.

I left under tense circumstances; their frustration had become palpable when it became clear I wasn't the "packaged deal" they had hoped for.

We continued to see each other every few years when I visited, but by then, I understood that I was never meant to stay in the pill-popping, hard-drinking, gambling-fueled life that Las Vegas offered anyone willing to accept the mission. My path was leading me somewhere else—toward college, stability, a career, marriage, and children.

Over time, we found peace in our friendship, but the sadness never fully left, and the debt felt unpaid. Did I play a part in his self-destruction? Could I have stopped it? His death left a deep sense of brokenness in me—a lingering guilt that I had somehow been complicit in his slow decline.

I felt like I owed him my life—but in the end, I couldn't give enough of myself to save him. Not from the yellowing jaundice or the bloating that marked his liver's final surrender. Not from the pills and alcohol that had hollowed him out, just as they've hollowed out so many across America.

This wasn't just his story—it was all of ours. Far too many of my childhood friends were lost to the same death spiral of addiction, shame, and silent judgment. A cycle no one talks about until it's too late.

The hungry ghost of this epidemic is relentless—feeding on pain, devouring futures. And it never stops at just one.

The cruelest part is that it makes a person feel invincible, like they can do anything—until the body finally cries mercy, and then comes the funeral procession.

He passed away just before I began my healing journey—during the pandemic, when even grief had to stand six feet away. There was no funeral, no gathering, no shared remembrance to honor his brief, complicated life. Just silence. And absence.

But he visited me in other ways. I felt his presence late at night while brushing my teeth, staring into the mirror. It struck me as strange at the time—but in hindsight, it made perfect sense. That was the only moment I really looked at myself—past the fog of the nightly beer buzz I'd come to depend on. Maybe he was trying to warn me. Maybe he was still trying to save me.

I carried the guilt for years—tight, silent, like a private punishment I thought I deserved. But the medicine doesn't let you lie. It took me to the root of my pain and asked me to forgive the girl who couldn't save anyone—because she was still trying to survive herself.

He never came to me in ceremony. Not once. And I mourned that absence as much as I mourned him. I wanted a proper goodbye. A chance to express gratitude—for his loyalty, his bravery, and his belief in me when I couldn't see my own worth.

He was skinny as a rail, without a trace of muscle—but he was the strongest kind of hero. The kind who showed up. The kind who looked an asshole in the eyes and said, "No more."

The kind who knew what love looked like—and fought like hell for it.

"HOME AGAIN"
Michael Kiwanuka

CHAPTER 8

GECKOS, RATS AND ROMEO

When I was 14, my mom left Chump. The aftermath of his destruction left us hollow—walking shadows of our former selves. One day, she sat me down and said her job was transferring, so we'd be moving. But I knew the truth: this wasn't about a job. Leaving Chump—and Nevada—was an act of survival.

We had already paid the price. My brother had been the human sacrifice, and the weight of that loss clung to us like a second skin—an unshakable reminder of Chump's darkness.

Our next stop: Saipan, a remote island in the South Pacific. Distant. Foreign. Unfamiliar. It would become our refuge, our desperate attempt to outrun the wreckage he left behind.

We were always moving, as if being hunted—but this time felt different. The urgency wasn't rooted in restlessness. It was about escape. The move to Saipan puzzled me. My mom's company had an opening for an office manager, so she accepted the position without hesitation. And just like that, we packed up and left—again.

Throughout my childhood, I lived in more homes than I can even recall as an adult. Each place was just a temporary stop, where I never quite felt at home. I learned early on not to settle in, to keep my sense of belonging at arm's length. Attachment was a weakness I couldn't afford to let myself feel. Staying ready for the next move was easier and less painful than becoming too attached to anyone or anything I might leave behind.

Rat bastard Chump kept our animals, and the guilt of leaving them behind gnawed at me. I couldn't protect them. It felt like escaping a war-torn village, saving the people while abandoning the animals to fend for themselves in the wreckage.

Being uprooted again stung, but leaving Allen and Marla, my best friends, was the hardest part. Allen had taken it the worst—we held each other and cried what felt like endless tears. He alone had shielded me from Chump; this meant everything. I was the guardian of the animals, and Allen was my protector. We were torn away from those roles. It was a heavy burden to bear. Our teenage hearts hung heavy as one.

When we landed on Saipan, it felt like I had arrived at the crossroads of paradise and purgatory.

After 26 hours of travel—departing from Las Vegas, then passing through Japan and Guam—we finally descended onto a tiny strip of land cresting out of the ocean. The final flight arrived late, its landing lights illuminating a runway so short it felt like we might skid straight into the water.

One of my mom's new co-workers met us at the airport, loading us into a Jeep and weaving through the narrow back roads toward a duplex buried deep in the jungle, where we'd stay for the next month. The ride was a blur of foreign experiences—pitch darkness framing lush greenery, the deafening symphony of insects delivering an otherworldly welcome, and the bone-rattling dirt roads so unforgiving that anything over 20 mph felt like a gamble.

Our driver, a man in his mid-50s, turned back with a grin and shouted, "If you drive 80 mph, you'll miss the bumps entirely!" It sounded like local wisdom, but we never dared to put it to the test. In our rusted-out Suzuki Samurai, every ride felt like an exercise in survival—we weren't entirely convinced the floorboard wouldn't drop out beneath us.

In Saipan, I stepped into a world that felt utterly foreign. The sticky humidity wrapped around me like an unwelcome embrace, as my long hair clung to my skin in defiant rebellion.

The duplex itself was simple—white walls, sparse furnishings, and island-themed decor that was intended to soften the unfamiliarity. Geckos scurried across the ceiling, their tiny bodies always threatening to plummet onto me in my sleep, while strange spiders lurked in the corners of my room, watching.

I had been ripped from the dry, sprawling suburbs of Las Vegas and dropped onto a claustrophobic tropical island, a lonely speck in the vast expanse of the South Pacific. The contrast was jarring—so was the realization that there was no going back. I checked my pants pockets every morning for the geckos that had taken up residence, as if they, too, had joined an imaginary witness protection program. They, too, were hiding.

My mom enrolled me in a private Catholic school, where I was equally unfamiliar with the language and the religion. Morning drop-offs felt more like a beach vacation than the traditional school. On the way we'd make a pit stop at a small shack across the street where fresh cinnamon-sugar donuts became my breakfast staple, with fried plantains tucked into sandwich bags as my go-to snack. It was a sugary lifeline in a world that felt entirely foreign.

The school had a strict uniform policy, but even in the required white and blue, I stuck out like a sore thumb. My dirty blonde hair and pale skin marked me as different—a Caucasian girl, sweating uncomfortably through her uniform, grasping for fragments of the native tongue.

The church attached to the school held all the ritual and pageantry of a traditional Catholic Mass, a grand display of robes, incense, and rehearsed reverence. I imagined the God I had once felt close to stifling a yawn, just as bored as I was by the endless formality. Attending those required services felt lifeless, as if everyone was just going through the motions, repeating words that had long since lost their meaning. My mind would drift, inventing ways to cut the service time in half by stripping away the layers of ceremony and pomp. Did we really need the stiff procession, the droning chants, and the same tired readings? Was it necessary to share a cup of wine, eat stale bread, and listen to a sermon in Latin that meant nothing to me?

It seemed far more efficient—and far more sacred—to simply fall to my knees, clasp my hands, and talk to God. No intermediaries, no rituals, no spectacle. Just a direct line, unfiltered and honest. I had felt God before, not in the echoing halls of that church but in quiet moments, in whispered prayers, in the unspoken knowing that I was heard.

Making friends felt impossible at first. Many classmates regarded me skeptically; I was the new white girl. Some of them even pretended to "teach" me Chamorro. Eager to fit in, I repeated what they taught me, only to find myself swiftly sent to the office for unknowingly saying the worst curse words in the language. *I quickly learned not to trust these lessons unless I needed to refer to a mother's vagina.* The first couple of months felt impossible to bear.

Our daily lessons were taught by nuns and priests in the school's open-air classrooms. English was the primary language, but conversations frequently slipped into Chamorro, leaving me nodding along in feigned understanding. The classrooms had sparse decorations— exposed to the elements, nothing seemed to withstand the relentless humidity, torrential rains, or the occasional typhoon. Even the walls seemed wiser, and less attached.

During those first challenging months, I found an unlikely confidant in a Spanish nun who became one of my closest friends. In a strange twist of fate, just a year earlier I had seriously considered becoming a nun myself—spending much of my free time reading the Bible and imagining a life devoted to spiritual service. Meeting her felt like a reflection of the path I almost chose—my closest encounter with a woman who had dedicated her life to God. At first, I feared she might sense or somehow detect the dirtiness my stepfathers had inflicted upon me, as if God Himself might tip her off. I was beyond saving. Against all odds, our friendship blossomed. I suspect she needed me as much as I needed her.

She walked with a slight slump, her short grey hair covered by a nun's veil, and simple glasses giving her an unassuming air and a crucifix proudly hanging from her neck. Yet, beneath that modest exterior was a woman of profound emotional and spiritual depth. Speaking with her felt like chatting with the most popular girl in high school, someone who, by sheer force of character, could make you feel seen.

They relegated our Spanish class to a cramped broom closet, probably because it was the least popular language choice. The windowless room had only a cheap plywood table; its atmosphere craved light conversation. We would sit with our Spanish books open in front of us, but they served more as props than tools. Almost every session devolved into sharing our lives instead—our habits, our challenges, our gossip, and our humanity.

At first, our conversations were cautious, like dipping our toes into the shallow end of a pool. "Good morning, Sister. How was your weekend?" I'd ask when entering the classroom. She'd respond with a calm recounting of her days: daily chores, working alongside her sisters, and time spent in prayer.

Then she'd turn the question back to me. My answers were far simpler. Hiked with Mom, wrote to mainland friends, then routine stuff.

As time went on, we waded deeper, sharing the struggles of living on a small island, the paths that had brought us to our current crossroads, and our individual relationships with God.

"Katie, please tell me about America and what it's like. I've always dreamt of going," she said one day. Her question, a quiet admittance of a dream beyond her devotion to God, took us far from the safe confines of small talk.

"I've lived in Oregon and Nevada. I'll describe that life. Then, will you tell me about Spain?"

Her face softened, and in that moment, I glimpsed a part of her she rarely let anyone see. Her family had always expected her to devote her life to the church, to their faith. At 19, she and her sisters had accepted what they saw as their destiny.

Yet, through our conversations, I caught fragments of another life—the life she might have chosen, had fate and familial expectations not sealed her path. These fleeting glimpses of a different life lingered subtly in her stories, unspoken and fragile. There was a boy that she had loved in school, friends that had charted a different course, and separation from the country she loved. Forty years later, she reflected on the people and life that she had sacrificed.

I told her muted stories of my life—the cruelty of a stepdad, the jagged edges of a childhood stolen. I didn't tell her the despicable slurs that he called me out of respect for her position and the delicate balance of our conversation. But I left enough details, carefully chosen and deliberately placed, for her to follow the breadcrumbs of my life.

My true talent lay in hiding the rawest truths in the spaces between my words, in the weight of the unspoken. Years had taught me to reveal selectively, safeguarding my vulnerabilities. We discussed the defining split in our timelines—the loss and unyielding, and the questions born from walking a life we were never empowered to choose.

We kept our books open as a facade in case anyone interrupted, but our minds were far from Spanish conjugations. Instead, we unearthed pieces of each other's souls. She missed Spain as terribly as I missed the US mainland, and, in our shared loneliness, we found an unexpected solace.

That tiny room with its oppressive walls and stale air became a sanctuary. More than an educational respite, it united two lonely hearts.

When a beloved priest faced accusations of harming children at the school and church, I turned to her first.

"Sister, have you heard the news about Father?"

They had been friends, and out of respect for her, I wanted to give her the space to share her thoughts first—to process the shocking news in her own way.

She looked at me, her expression clouded with disbelief. "Katie, I just don't understand what happened—or what this all means. How could he do that?" Her voice carried a weight I had never heard before, a tone of quiet defeat.

Father had been a boisterous, comedic presence, the unofficial heart of the school. He was everywhere—in our classrooms, in our hallways, in our memories as a former beacon of laughter.

But after the revelation and the fallout—not just about him, but about multiple priests—we were left standing in the wreckage of something we once trusted without question.

We were all deeply impacted.

It reshaped and shattered her worldview, her trust in authority, her faith in righteousness, and everything she once believed to be inherently good.

For me, I had already broken ties with God, and this only reinforced my belief that it had been the right decision. But years later, I would come to understand this was never God's doing. The horror belonged to men who distorted faith to feed their power—who used the sacred as a shield for the profane. The blame was theirs alone. God had never been part of it. In fact, God had been weeping with us the whole time.

From an outsider's perspective, and as someone who had not grown up in the church, I saw with unsettling clarity how often God's name was used to justify the deeds of the devil.

Our relationship with faith shifted in ways I couldn't fully grasp at the time. In an instant, she seemed different—broken in a way I had never seen before. Her hair looked strikingly whiter, her posture more stooped, and her eyes dimmed. It was as if something vital within her had been extinguished.

I don't know if she questioned the faith, she had spent a lifetime cultivating, but even with my own experiences of abuse, the abrupt fracture in our belief system was undeniable.

It left us all wondering—who, if anyone, was truly good at heart? And could we ever again trust the institutions we once held sacred?

After school, I'd walk half a mile to my mom's office, or tutor English to Korean students at the small shop next door. The mother, often covered in leeches, would open the door with blood gently trickling down her arms, as if it were the most ordinary thing in the world—a remedy for whatever ailment she believed plagued her.

Safely walking through town felt like a victory, given the common sight of nine-year-olds driving old Nissan trucks on the main road. Law enforcement family connections ensured protection; Saipan locals commonly boasted such ties.

The island itself was a mesmerizing paradox of beauty and peril. Crystal-clear waters lapped softly at the shore, while palm trees swayed in the crosswinds, their fronds whispering secrets of the sea. Yet, scattered amid this tropical paradise were haunting relics of history—a half-submerged World War II tank, hand grenades, and cutlery rusted in caves and along shores—a silent reminder of battles long past.

The reef, jagged and unyielding, stood as both guardian and warning. It formed a natural barrier, keeping sharks and barracudas at bay within its fortress-like embrace. But beyond its edge lay the abyss of the Mariana Trench—where the brave, the reckless, and the doomed alike tempted fate.

Whispered tales circulated of shark attacks and the ill-fated nurses who, after one drink too many had floated past the reef into the ocean's merciless grip. These stories kept even the boldest islanders grounded in their respect for the ocean's deadly mysteries. On land, there were no poisonous snakes to fear, but the waters offered a stark reminder that paradise always comes with its own set of dangers.

Mom and I often found ourselves at a local brick bar in the evenings. It was a favored haunt for construction workers and other newcomers to the island. The place buzzed with a rough camaraderie, a shared understanding among misfits and drifters, where the few Caucasians blended in with locals over cold beers and familiar tunes.

Every now and then, the bartender or a generous regular would slide a frosty beer my way, treating me less like a teenager and more like an honorary adult. The adults, perhaps loosened by their drinks or amused by my presence, would sometimes press spare change into my palm, encouraging me to try my luck at the gambling machines— a fleeting thrill, and a brief escape from the island's slow, relentless rhythm.

Built of sturdy brick, the bar wasn't just a watering hole—it doubled as a fortress when typhoons rolled in. When storms loomed, we'd hunker down inside, swapping stories and playing cards as the wind howled and rain lashed against the walls. Those stormy nights, thick with the scent of beer and salt air, became a strange kind of sanctuary. In the glow of flickering lanterns and neon signs, we found comfort in the chaos, laughing, drinking, and riding out the storm like it was just another song on the jukebox.

Typhoon nights were some of the best nights. There was a reckless freedom in surrendering to the inevitable, in drinking our fill while the world unraveled outside. It was terrifying, for sure, but maybe all natural disasters would be easier to bear if people had cards in their hands, music in the background, and a bottle to pass around. Oblivion, camaraderie, and the simple act of living in the moment dulled the edges of fear. In those hours, we weren't just surviving; we were alive.

Stray dogs freely roamed the island, scavenging for scraps and lazing in the heat. It wasn't uncommon to see a pair mating right in the middle of a dirt road, oblivious to passing traffic. If someone hit a dog, we'd load it up and offer it to the workers crammed into squalid barracks, where a fresh meal—no matter the source—was always welcomed with gratitude.

Saipan's population was a blend of Filipino laborers, a handful of Caucasians, and the indigenous Chamorro people. Few outsiders realized that the Mariana Islands were a U.S. territory, or that remnants of World War II still lay scattered across the lush landscape.

This period was difficult. By the time I was 14, I had moved more times than I cared to count—Bend, Prineville, Redmond, Silverton, Corvallis, Boulder City, Henderson, and Hillsboro. Town to town, house to house, I learned adaptability out of necessity.

A month into school, I landed the role of Juliet in the school play. Tom, a tall, dark-haired Chamorro guy with an infectious energy, was cast as Romeo.

The next morning, a dozen roses appeared on my desk from him. From that moment on, we were inseparable.

His family owned the island's only major grocery store, and suddenly, through this unexpected romance, I felt something shift. Where I had once been an outsider, I was now tolerated by the locals, maybe even accepted.

I also found friendship with Kimberly and Samantha, two other Caucasian girls navigating life on the island. Kimberly's mom worked for the U.S. Census, and Samantha, whose mother had long since disappeared, had spent years on the island with her alcoholic father. Together, we carved out a space for ourselves in a place that never quite felt like home.

The island was also a haven for lost souls. A Vietnam veteran had fled to Saipan, hoping to escape the grip of his PTSD. Australian shop owners arrived in search of perfect waves, only to be chased out of the water by sharks. Drifters and wanderers found solace in Saipan's remoteness, using the island's beauty and mystery as a veil behind which to disappear. Here, the world forgot them, and for many, that was exactly the point.

After a couple of months, I settled in. Island life slowed. It became peaceful, and beautifully simple. Family, love, and food were at the heart of everything. Gatherings, whether on the beach or in someone's home—were a feast of indulgent flavors and unguarded affection. Life on the island revolved around food—chicken kelaguen, whole roasted pig, and heaping plates of red rice. People chewed betel nuts, their teeth stained deep red, and spat onto the ground, leaving streaks of crimson in the dust. Crowds of men gathered around makeshift arenas, tossing down bets as roosters with sharp blades fastened to their legs tore into each other in the frenzy of a cockfight.

I learned to move at the rhythm of "island time," where urgency didn't exist, and the outside world felt like a distant, irrelevant hum. Time didn't hold the same weight there. The only drama that mattered was the kind that unfolded within the island's borders—its own universe, untouched by time. Clocks were mere suggestions.

I started working at a pizza shop to make ends meet, honing my skills by folding waffle cones and scooping ice cream. I worked alongside a Filipino woman who boasted about her 21 children, though I could never keep their names straight. Most of my co-workers viewed me as a novelty—someone who had never known the true poverty they had. Despite that, I listened to their stories and showed interest in their language and lives.

Rats dominated the island—they were small, but in charge. They infested the dumpsters behind the restaurant, and I would throw bags of trash from a distance, watching as the rats scattered in every direction, sometimes running over my feet or legs. My upper strength increased from the rat-run challenge. Worse yet, the movie theater's rats brazenly grabbed food from viewers' hands.

One day, a group of us skipped school and hopped on a cheap charter flight to the neighboring island of Tinian. The pilot casually asked for our weights, and for a moment, I questioned my safety. I sat in the co-pilot's seat, gripping the door slightly ajar for the entire flight, silently praying to a God I no longer believed in.

We spent the day swimming on an isolated beach, completely untethered from the world, half-joking about whether the pilot would come back for us. He did, and we made our way home, but the day stayed with me.

There was something about that string of remote islands that made me feel both insignificant and completely free. The beach was ours; the crystal-blue waters sang of a land before time, and for a moment, it felt like we could simply disappear into the landscape.

Yet, back on solid ground, nothing ever stayed still. Within a year, we cycled through three residences—a duplex, a basement apartment, and finally, a place where I had my own bedroom. With each move, I adapted, settling in just long enough to call it home before packing up again.

But that last place was different. The view stretched out into the jungle—lush, endless, alive. For the first time, I didn't want to leave.

However, just as I began to feel rooted in Saipan, my mom dropped the news—we were moving to Idaho.

After a year on the island, I had finally started to belong. The locals no longer saw me as an outsider. I had adjusted to the climate, the culture, and the slow rhythm of island life. I had found solace, a hint of belonging, even affection.

Now, it was all being ripped away.

A bitterness invaded me, sharp and unwelcome. I placed all the blame on my mom. I had no rights, no decision, and no vote. It didn't matter how much I wanted to stay—the choice had already been made.

I swallowed my anger, but it swelled in my chest, burning. Hot tears rolled down my face as I sat in silent rebellion, furious at a world where I had no control.

On the flight back to the mainland, I pressed my forehead against the window, mourning the life I had left behind.

With "Nothing Compares 2 U" playing through my Walkman, I cried until the batteries died.

Until the island faded from view.

Then, all that was left was the hum of the plane and the ache of another lost home.

I arrived in Idaho with a firm resolve: I would not belong. My heart was still in Saipan, and as far as I was concerned, this stop was only temporary. That island was mine, and I was part of it.

But here I was again, a new school, a new house, another fresh start. By this point, the endless cycle of packing, moving, and adjusting had worn me thin. I was exhausted. I loathed the transient life, the constant uprooting, and the inevitable small talk that always led to the same question:

"Are your parents in the military?"

My go-to response was a dry, "No, just a mom who likes to move around," masking my fatigue with sarcasm. The truth was, I craved permanence—something steady, and certain. But stability remained just out of reach, always teasing, always slipping away before I could grasp it.

In Idaho, I took a job at a fast-food restaurant, determined to save every penny for a one-way ticket back to Saipan. The uniforms were hideous, and the endless grease meant I never had to worry about moisturizing, but I didn't care. I was a girl on a mission, eagerly picking up everyone's shifts to reach my goal.

At just 15 years old, I was convinced I could make it on my own—that I could escape the constant moving, break free, and build my own life.

Tom and I tried to stay in touch, but the high cost of phone calls made it nearly impossible. (Remember, this was pre-internet.) Still, I was determined. With my mom's permission, I bought my ticket, packed my bags, and boarded a flight—alone.

I had no intention of staying on the mainland. I was 15, on my own, and ready to define my future—regardless of my age, the obstacles, or the risks.

Six months after leaving Saipan, I returned.

No parents. No safety net. Just me.

I stayed with my friend in her bleak, suffocating house, where her father, a long-time alcoholic, spiraled deeper into his addiction. My presence seemed to fuel his drinking, and with it, his abusive behavior escalated.

The house itself mirrored the chaos inside. Toilet use was often avoided due to unreliable plumbing. It felt like a grim metaphor for our lives, everyone holding their shit in until it inevitably exploded.

Reality hit hard: Saipan, once my beacon of hope, was no longer a place where I could build a future. The burden proved too much; I booked a return flight. The weight of it all became undeniable, and I knew I had no choice but to get on that flight back. This departure felt essential for survival.

While I waited for the return to the States, I picked up smoking, and when I wasn't working, I spent most of my time holed up in my friend's room, chain-smoking cigarettes and hiding—from her father, from the chaos, and from life itself. I had expected things to be as good or better upon my return; I'd painted an optimistic picture. I had mistakenly hoped for a welcoming return to the island, reminiscent of our departure. But it wasn't the same.

It was clear the island had stayed the same, but the people were different. Tom's focus had shifted; he was involved with someone new. The island's once warm and magical embrace felt distant, almost indifferent. The magic that had captivated me had vanished. My youthful vision had proven to be a fantasy.

Growing up with such instability gifted me adaptability, though not without a cost. I became a chameleon; I learned to blend into every environment, and fade into the background just to survive. But even in the silence of those lonely years, I dreamed—of belonging, of making a city feel like home, of planting roots and of building something that lasted.

Years passed between those lonely nights in Saipan and the moment I finally built a life in Idaho. The journey wasn't linear, but each detour brought me closer to the stability I craved. What began as survival slowly evolved into intention.

So, I did.

I got to know my neighbors. I dug my hands into the soil of my garden. I volunteered, gave back, and invested in the community that embraced me. And in return, I found what I had longed for my entire life—love, connection, and a safe harbor to finally call my own.

For some, uncertainty and instability become a catalyst for change. For others, they become a trap—an endless cycle of repetition. But no matter how they shape us, they serve as reminders that transformation is born from creation, not circumstance.

Even before my year of healing, I had attained a stability I had never thought was possible. A home, a future, real support—all the things that had once felt unattainable were suddenly mine. It became the foundation for rebuilding love, hope, and resilience.

Yet, even with all I built, something still lingered deep within me—an ache that refused to be ignored.

But even as I settled into adulthood, something unresolved lingered deep within me. It wasn't until an ayahuasca ceremony years later that the memory surfaced—so vivid, it was as if I'd been transported back in time to Saipan.

I was 15 years old, sitting in Samantha's room. Her father raged in an alcoholic blur, his voice slurring through the thin walls. I sat on her bed, exhausted, and overwhelmed, asking myself: *How did I get here?*

Moving to Saipan alone at 15, what was I thinking? Why had I spent the evening deep-frying food in an ugly uniform just to land here?

I saw my younger self, utterly worn down by the weight of not belonging. A girl who had already endured a lifetime of abuse, carrying an insurmountable loneliness. And yet, somehow, she had made it here—to a life she had never imagined possible.

The medicine brought me back to that girl—sitting on that daybed, smoking a cigarette, fearful and confused. I saw her clearly, a young soul forced to grow up far too quickly.

She had believed she was taking a stand—tired of moving, convinced that, from now on, her choices would dictate her life. But in the end, the mission failed. Her remaining pride suffered. And Saipan, with its quiet wisdom, had gently but unmistakably let her know it was time to move on.

During the ceremony, I did what that 15-year-old girl had needed most:

I sat beside her. I held her as she cried. And we cried together.

Sometimes, that's all you can do—allow the tears to flow, honor the pain of the past, and give yourself the permission to heal.

That 15-year-old girl unknowingly showed immense bravery, offering a gift to my previous, fragmented selves. She had grit—an adventurous spirit that refused to be extinguished, and a glimmer of hope even in her darkest moments. She embraced the lessons that came with failed attempts and faced adversities no one should face alone.

Sitting on that daybed, she caught fleeting glimpses of a brighter future—a future the universe had always intended for her.

It was waiting there, beyond the cigarette smoke haze.

Patiently.

I only needed the resolve to step through that door, board the plane, and start again.

"HEAL"

Tom Odell

CHAPTER 9

COKE, CHEEZ WHIZ AND GRANDMA'S ASHES

My husband and I parked the car and walked toward my aunt's house. My cousin Roy came flying towards us on a kid's stolen BMX bike. The scene was straight out of a movie; looking strung out, and short of breath, he skidded to a halt so that a cloud of dust billowed around us, forcing us to clear our airways.

There was no time for pleasantries. Roy looked at us with wild eyes and asked, "Have you seen or heard the cops?" My husband and I exchanged glances, then said, "No."

With a quick, "Good to see you, Katie," he was off again, pedaling furiously, his adult legs working overtime on a kid's undersized bike. My husband, who had only heard the legends of my cousins' escapades, stood wide-eyed. Roy's grand entrance did not disappoint.

Wearing a weathered Levi's denim jacket, he tore down the alley, bunny-hopped the railroad tracks, and disappeared into the sunset like a chaotic antihero.

I turned to my husband and said, "That's my cousin Roy, by the way."

These moments left a deeper imprint than I realized—etching early lessons about drugs, escape, and the kind of high that never really heals.

Later, as we sat at the kitchen table drinking coffee with my aunt, the sound of footsteps echoed from above the garage. We sipped our coffees and kept the conversation light, while pretending not to notice. We knew the unspoken rule: act as though we weren't aware of the person above us, moving, trying to remain undetected. But we all knew my cousin Ryan was somewhere in the bowels of the house, lurking and lying low, doing his best to evade being found or arrested.

The last time I had visited Ryan's mother, my Aunt Sharly in Hillsboro, her sons had been living at her house. As far as the police, her husband, or anyone else were concerned, they hadn't existed in years. Most of the family preferred to act as though my cousins didn't exist—at least until their names crackled over the police radio scanners.

We all played along as if everything was normal, but they were the family's secret—hidden away in attics or stashed at safe houses, out of sight but never out of mind. That's what we did as a family—we kept our mouths shut, turned a blind eye, let the crazy-making continue, and communicated in our own unspoken family Morse code.

Aunt Sharly had always struggled to navigate raising her teenage boys. Their father had been a deadbeat from day one, leaving her overwhelmed and uncertain. In their teenage years, she had placed them in the foster care system.

Sharly was the original shorty badass, standing just under five feet tall. Her cropped black hair exuded a "don't mess with me" confidence.

It made her look more masculine than feminine—and she carried herself with an aura that commanded respect.

The bitterness that seemed to emanate from her often overshadowed her loving kindness. Despite her height, no one dared underestimate her. She wasn't a woman to be trifled with, and her sharp, dead-aimed glare brought the boldest of mortals to their knees. Losing a limb—or your dignity—seemed like a real possibility if you crossed her.

Sharly and I grew close during my teenage years, our bond sealed by an unspoken pact. Her brand of love went to her rescue dogs, she had less love for humans. With Sharly, the rules were clear: we didn't talk about Ryan, his brother Roy, or the financial and emotional ruin they'd left in their wake.

It was a fragile peace I adhered to for years—until I broke it.

As teenagers, a man who had offered them foster care, a house, and food had raped Ryan and Roy. Sharly, my grandmother, and the Oregon penal system had taken turns as the reluctant team captains in the aftermath of raising Ryan and Roy well into their middle age.

In my early teens, before Sharly's divorce, I spent some summers in the hills outside Hillsboro, Oregon. Sharly was married to "Fib," who owned expansive property near a rock quarry deep in the Oregon mountains, with no neighbors for miles. Despite being surrounded by nature and having everything a grown man desired, the house carried an oppressive heaviness that lingered like a dark shadow.

Fib surpassed reality. His nickname came from the glorious fact that he never let the truth impede a good story. With a weathered face, an uncanny ability to make money, and a knack for spotting a worthy investment, Fib was the quintessential rogue. He was the man who had crashed his plane twice and walked away without a scratch, wearing the experience like a badge of honor and embarrassment. Upon completion of his replacement plane, he'd offer airplane rides, prompting everyone to say, "Oh, that would be nice," while never intending to risk our lives.

Fib had a way of pulling you into his world. He'd have you jump into his "rig" to listen to his fantastical, often exaggerated tales, all while gripping an Olympia Stubby. His beloved Dachshund, Jenny, was always by his side—his true main gal. Jenny would perch on the middle console, claiming ownership of both the truck and Fib, ready to bite anyone who dared enter their sacred space. His storytelling and energy were magnetic, the kind that swept people up, no matter how far-fetched they seemed.

Years later, when I visited him as an adult, Fib took a particular liking to my husband. He would ply him with drinks until they were both drunk, then they would climb into heavy machinery, convinced they could operate it better under the influence. Fib's spirit burned unrestrained, seemingly fueled by his drunken revelry.

Each morning started with a tactical sweep of the hallway, on high alert for the tiny turds, Sharly's squad of purse-sized dogs had lovingly scattered like offerings. I often spent summers riding four-wheelers with Fib across his expansive property. I'd return with poison oak or ivy clinging to my skin—and always have a story to tell.

One year, not realizing I'd been exposed to poison oak, I immersed myself in the hot tub. Big mistake. The rash that followed was so severe the doctor glanced at me before tossing ointment my way, as if words couldn't address the hot mess I'd made of my skin.

Despite the natural beauty surrounding us, the house was suffocating. In the living room, a punch bag stood installed, treated like a piece of furniture, a fitting symbol of the tense and combative energy that filled the space. My troubled cousins, Ryan and Roy, along with Sharly's sharp, heavy energy, created a tension that made the walls close in—on themselves and on us. Roy and Ryan drifted in and out during those summers, their explosive outbursts and escalating drug use impossible to ignore.

Even Fib, with his laid-back demeanor, seemed to recognize the daunting reality ahead: the road was far too long and treacherous to navigate the chaos of two boys teetering on the edge of adulthood and a mother who refused to discuss the truth.

Years later, under the strain of it all, Sharly and Fib's marriage fell apart. The weight of raising troubled teens, the emotional toll, and the suffocating atmosphere proved too much to bear. Sharly moved to a small house in town, bringing her trail of rescued dogs and lost boys along with her.

When I was in my early teen years, summers were a time of limbo, spent shuttling between my grandmothers in Central Oregon and my Aunt Sharly near Portland. In Bend, there was Grandma Betty, my biological father's mother. In Prineville, Grandma Wanda, my mother's mom, awaited. These summer visits opened doors to worlds as contrasting as light and dark—day and night.

In my early teens, I would board the Greyhound bus on my own, crisscrossing the state of Oregon to land at the doorstep of whichever family member would take me off my mother's hands.

Grandma Wanda's diminutive frame, four feet ten inches tall, was adorned with a silver chain holding her reading glasses; she needed them to scrutinize her aging skin under a magnifying mirror. Her hair was translucent white, so fine that the redness of her scalp shone through like a beacon. Her skin often bore fresh sores, which, if you didn't know better, might lead you to suspect she was a crack

addict. She wasn't—but my cousin, who lived in that house, consumed enough drugs for the entire family, including a small horse. I
used to wonder if the cocaine particles floating through the air had
somehow contributed to Wanda's incessant picking.

Despite this, Wanda had a defiant flair for boldness. She wore massive pieces of turquoise jewelry that seemed to weigh more than she
did, paired with polyester checkered pants that only she could pull
off—her homage to the 70s. But her artistry was where she shone.
She painted stunning scenes of Central Oregon—an old, weathered
barn leaning in the wind, a Juniper tree twisting up from the sage-
brush, or a sprawling landscape that captured the essence of the high
desert. Her work was a love letter to the region, each painting reflecting her connection to the land.

Grandma Wanda could spend hours hunched over her magni-
fied mirror, plucking chin hair while chain-smoking cigarettes. Once
she'd had a few glasses of wine, the conversation would circle back
to the same topic: my grandfather's abrupt departure from the family. With the clutches of her tweezers still holding a plucked chin
hair, she'd lament, in her wine-induced righteous indignation, that
she just couldn't understand why he left her. After a long drag from
her cigarette, she'd declare, once again, that he'd cheated and been
"lured away" by the other woman.

As a sober 13-year-old, I found myself cast as her unwilling confidant. During MTV commercial breaks, I would dispense my sage
advice, aware that my role required always casting her as the victim. In
the 80s, MTV was my sanctuary, and music videos were my religion. I
lived for the moments when a new release would drop, it was a sacred
ritual that demanded full attention before any conversation could
resume. Grandma Wanda, ever patient, would sit nearby, plucking

her chin hair as she waited for my attention to return to her ongoing issues. It was an unspoken understanding; the music came first, and then we could dive back into the tangled threads of her laments.

The TV in the living room, an oversized 56-inch monstrosity with a wooden frame that made it as much a piece of furniture as an electronic device, was the heart of the house. Every night, Grandma Wanda and I would curl up in our well-worn chairs facing the screen, creating what I can only describe as an impromptu truth-speaking ceremony. The house was ramshackle—in need of fresh paint, roof repair, a feather duster, and a reprieve from the toxicity that seeped out of endless cigarettes and fractured lives.

Amid the glow of MTV videos and the haze of cigarette smoke, we'd dive into our nightly ritual of unpacking life's dramas. For her, it was the heartache of the past; for me, it was the rhythm and escape of music. Those nights became an odd sort of communion—two different lives intersecting over pop culture and personal confessions.

For most of my teenage years, Ryan, who was ten years my senior, lived with my grandma. The entire family knew that housing Ryan was the real reason my grandparents broke up—though there were plenty of other contributing factors. Ryan was wiry, with an air of contagious paranoia that seemed to follow him everywhere. His big lips, out of proportion to the rest of his face, gave him a mismatched appearance.

Watching Ryan grow up vibrant and full of potential, it was easy to imagine a different life for him—one where he chose a more conventional path. In my mind, I could see him with a steady job as a skilled tradesman, a loving wife, and children running through the yard. Instead, Ryan had chosen the path of 1980s excess, dedicating himself full-time to the hardest drugs imaginable. In those moments, it was hard not to wonder what might have been—what life he might have built if he had chosen love, purpose, or sobriety over addiction. Instead, Ryan's habits confined his world to haze, leaving the rest of us to navigate the fallout.

Summers often revolved around Ryan's antics, as if the rest of us were the sideshow to his main act. He'd send Grandma Wanda on Cheez Whiz runs, pocket her dwindling stash of turquoise jewelry, or accuse me of making expensive phone calls—just to deflect blame. Ryan had been the one dialing 1-900 numbers geared toward straight male callers, but somehow, despite my being a 13-year-old girl, Grandma saw me as the culprit. Caught in Ryan's web of misdirection, she'd call my mother in fury, insisting I'd racked up hundreds of dollars in charges. I knew how absurd it was, but in that chaotic household, defending myself felt like shouting in a void. As one of the few people granted access to the house's dark inner sanctum of debauchery, Ryan made the most of his time by orchestrating phone sex escapades and pawning anything that wasn't bolted to the floor.

Ryan wrestled with whether he was straight or gay, an uncertainty that seemed to compound the weight he carried, making his escape into drugs both inevitable and tragic. From the abuse, Ryan spent his hours questioning his sexuality in a state of confusion, brokenness and uncertainty. He trudged the path as a deeply, broken soul.

His days were long and uneventful; he remained unemployed by choice. He passed the time shooting up heroin, then emerging in the mornings wearing nothing but his tighty-whities. Scratching his crotch, he'd stagger into the kitchen, to say *"Where's my fucking Coke and Cheez Whiz?"* The tone was dripping with accusation, as if someone had stolen it—rather than admitting he'd consumed it all day before in a drug-induced haze. I'd shout to my grandma that

Ryan was awake, and it was time to head to the store. That was our ritual for starting a new day.

Ryan's relentless cries for more processed food meant my grandmother, and I often piled into her boat of a car, heading straight for the nearest convenience store. At our height, we could barely see over the dashboard—looking like a pair of kids who swiped their mom's car keys and were about to joyride through the neighborhood.

Grandma would light one of her signature "More" cigarettes—those ultra-long, thin marvels with a talent for holding onto the most improbable ash. Somehow, that cigarette's ash remained intact for the entire journey, defying potholes and bumps like a miracle of modern engineering.

Even her forgetfulness to put the car into park at the store—resulting in a jarring curb check while the attendant clutched their chest in alarm—couldn't shake the cigarette's determination. That long ash held firm, defying gravity, chaos, and all odds until the very end of our journey.

Meanwhile, back home, Grandma's culinary specialty awaited: Kraft cheese and white bread sandwiches. No frills, no extras—just processed perfection with a side of ash for added texture. To avoid surprise seasoning from her notorious cigarette, I guarded coffee cups and glasses like treasures.

And yet, we survived. Maybe it was the "fortified" vitamins in the bread and cheese that kept us going, or maybe it was sheer stubbornness. Either way, there we were—bouncing over potholes, Grandma puffing away, and the ash at the tip of her cigarette defying gravity, refusing to break. A true testament to resilience—hers, mine, and even the cigarettes.

When he moved into my grandma's house, I had seen the newspaper articles Ryan had clipped out and taped to the back of his closet door—grim stories about the foster care teenage predator that altered his life forever. It was a chilling homage to the abuse he'd endured, immortalized on the door to remind him of the permanence of his trauma.

When we were much younger, my denim-jacket-wearing cousins exuded an effortless air of rebellion. They were the cool, older bad boys, their bedroom walls adorned with Led Zeppelin and neon-colored velvet pot posters—the fine art of 80s counterculture.

But as the years passed, I witnessed their transition—from typical teenage troublemakers to damaged souls. There was no safe passage to the other side of the abuse they had endured. For Ryan and Roy, the wounds ran too deep, shaping their lives in ways that no one could undo.

Because we were all victims of sexual abuse, we shared a bond of kinship. But it ran deeper—a connection forged as tortured souls. Casual conversations with Ryan often took surreal turns. He would break out his needle kit, sliding the needle into his vein as if it was the same as taking another sip of coffee. I would watch, frozen, as he shot up heroin, and to this day, I still close my eyes whenever a needle comes near anyone's skin.

Ryan would sometimes encourage me to join him in his drug use. I remain thankful for my polite refusal.

By my early teenage years, I had lived through enough to feel much older than my age. Ryan and I shared a close, complicated relationship. He tolerated me in his own way, and opened up about his experiences, sharing things I suspect he had told no one else. We traded stories, troubles, and secrets, forming an unspoken bond despite the chaos surrounding us.

It might sound strange, but through all of his lostness—and aside from offering me drugs—Ryan never laid a finger on me or spoke a cruel word. Despite my vulnerability, shaped by both my age and the life I'd lived, he treated me as an equal. It was a rare respect, born from shared pain and unspoken understanding, in a world where kindness was a luxury for us both.

In our own messed-up way, I cared and felt deep empathy for him. Because, in truth, I was lost too—maybe not as far gone as Ryan but lost enough to recognize the path he was on. That understanding created a bond between us, one forged in the shared weight of what we had endured.

Ryan became a living life lesson for me. He was a stark reminder of what could happen if I let the abuse consume me. If I too got pulled into that darkness, it could eat me alive. I could end up on drugs for life, in prison, or dead.

He showed me that, when life fucks you up, there's always a fork in the road. Ryan was a vivid, breathing example of the worst-case scenario. If the weight of it all breaks you, you might find yourself stuck—living with your grandma, sustained by Coke, Cheez Whiz, heroin, and ruin.

Beneath his grocery store demands and absentminded scrotum scratches, I saw a deeper raw pain—an internal struggle with his identity.

My grandma was also a certified teacher in life lessons. She showed me the cost of enabling a victim—how they can drain not just your savings, but also your life force. If you refuse to move forward after someone leaves you, clinging to denial and bitterness while avoiding accountability for your choices, life doesn't cut you any slack. Instead, it serves you a processed shit sandwich with a heaped side of "More" ash. And that's all you get.

One year, my cousin had the audacity to grow a thriving pot bush right in front of the mailbox. Although I had never used marijuana, I knew enough to recognize it—and it stuck out like a sore thumb against the high desert landscape.

In a small town where gossip spread like wildfire, it wasn't long before the mailman brought the news down to the local diner. Soon, everyone knew my grandmother was cultivating "the most beautiful pot plant this side of the Three Sisters Mountain range."

When my uncle caught wind of it, he stormed over and ripped the bush clean out of the ground. My grandmother, ever defensive, insisted that Ryan would never do such a thing. The absurdity of it all was that, after denying it had been him, she still marveled at his unexpected gardening skills—as if the plant itself stood as proof of his green thumb.

When the drug bust happened at my grandma's house, the family had had enough. They insisted that Ryan and my grandmother be separated. But my grandma wanted no part of it. No matter what anyone said, she remained loyal to him.

Over the years, Ryan ended up in prison, but even incarceration couldn't sever the bond between them. No drug bust or prison sentence could break the unshakable connection that bound them together for life.

Still, the family insisted that their mother, Sharly, take accountability and "do her time" for her role in the mess. While Ryan and my grandma were inseparable, the rest of the family had reached their breaking point.

It was around this time that I sided with the rest of the family. My grandmother was getting older, and I called Sharly to share my concerns. Sharly, ever loyal to her vow of silence about her boys, took my actions as a betrayal. In response, she severed ties with me in the cruelest way.

We had always been closer than most, which made her words cut deeper than I could have imagined. She told me to fuck off—that she was done with me. But she delivered it without a hint of compassion, not even a whisper. In an instant, she erased our years together.

After that conversation, I remember collapsing onto the bathroom floor, broken and weeping. It took me months to gather the pieces of my shattered heart. Despite knowing what she could be like with people, I had believed I was the one person who could speak out to her.

I could never understand how she could remain so cold, so unyielding, as a human being. Perhaps some things about people and their actions remain beyond our understanding. Maybe it was our shared blood that kept me trying to find connection—but aside from our mutual love of dogs, we were never alike.

If I had to guess, the events concerning her boys wounded her. Over the years, that wound in her soul must have festered, and even mentioning the situation felt like prodding at her wound. Her lashing out and alienating family members seemed to stem from the kind of repressed anger that brews when we refuse to confront the deep issues.

Some people perfect the art of denial. Others, like Ryan and me, find different ways to escape.

After years of refusing his pleas to try heroin, I finally gave in and tried LSD with him. I was just 13, and he reassured me, *"It'll be fine."* That night, Ryan perched himself on the roof, acting as a spotter with a flashlight, scanning for imaginary police officers while I spent hours combing through blades of grass below. It was my first experience with drugs—and the last time I ever did anything like that with him.

I did not know what drugs were or the long-term consequences they carried. I was too young to understand the weight of what I was stepping into.

As my grandmother neared the end of her life, Ryan stepped in to oversee the care of her well-earned but fragile health. In those last days, it was Ryan and Sharly—though mostly Ryan—by her side. They sneaked her cigarettes, kept watch over her, and spent hours together on the covered back patio, its fake plastic grass doubling as a convenient potty station for the dogs.

"The doctors say my lungs are clear," she would declare as she lit one of her cigarettes, standing near her red Dodge Neon. The Neon was an upgrade from the old boat of a car that had defined our store adventures, its vast interior carrying more memories than groceries.

My mom had wanted her to quit smoking, but for the rest of us, the truth was clear: the damage was done. She deserved to greet death on her own terms, surrounded by the habits and people who had defined her and brought her refuge.

Growing up, Ryan peppered his interactions with my grandmother with "fuck you's" and "fuck off's," tossing them out as casually as a kind greeting. Yet as the end approached, he softened. The hardened, balding drug addict seemed to understand the gravity of his role when the time came, and he rose to the occasion. I like to think he always knew how much she had sacrificed for him and all that he had taken from her. Their love was dysfunctional, but it was the only love either of them had ever known. My grandmother believed in Ryan until her final breath, and he knew she was his one-in-a-million.

In her last days, he honored her. He sat on the patio, fetched her water, and made sure she passed with as much peace as he could provide. The moments they shared were raw, imperfect, and human.

There's a strange comfort in the messiness of it all. After her passing, the same band of misfits who had drained her bank account and left her in financial ruin surrounded her. Yet, despite it all, they were her tribe. Bound by mutual tolerance of each other's quirks, shared idiosyncrasies, and buried secrets, they formed a bond that was broken but unyielding. In the end, they were her unlikely family—flawed, loyal, and as real as love gets in this imperfect world.

All those memories shaped me, opening my eyes in both the worst and most beneficial ways. I learned the damage caused by unspoken words, the toxicity of hidden emotion and the countless ways outside forces can fuck us up.

By the time I arrived at my grandmother's doorstep, the ravages of abuse had damaged me. Her house and my cousins were both par for the course and the worst-case scenario. Yet, through it all, I somehow remained in the tender-hearted clan—loving them, recognizing their wounds, even while knowing I didn't want to grow up to be like them.

I loved them. I moved forward, and I understood that, if I was going to make it out alive, I had no other option but to choose a different path.

Years later, when I used drugs on a frequent, almost regular basis, Ryan was the one to sound the family alarm. He delivered the news to my family as if he were a fallen hero, throwing himself on the sword for the greater good. But we both knew the truth. He had played a pivotal role in opening that door for me. In watching Ryan and my grandma's paths, I took the good and bad lessons with me. While I tried, I did not make it out unscathed.

My desensitization preceded my drug use. Drugs had become a familiar tool in my belt, a way to cope with the relentless onslaught of suffering—a trick I had learned from him, from all of them, even if neither of us ever spoke those words aloud.

I loved doing the right thing. But sometimes my quirky moral compass led me straight down south. I grew up perceiving all drugs as bad, but I didn't want to face my life—I didn't want to look at the past, the damage, or the toll it had taken. So, when I used drugs, it was always secretive and done with the utmost discretion. Then I'd wake up and go to college, or clean-up for my job, or step back into whatever role life had assigned me.

After trying LSD with my cousin, I stayed away from drugs for a few years. Eventually it was alcohol that opened that door for me. Drinking was acceptable, so when I moved to Saipan, I embraced it—sipping cocktails at the bar or sharing beers with friends on the beach.

After a couple of years of that, I picked up a cigarette, and with it, more doors opened. Ironically, it was the "acceptable" toxic substances—alcohol and cigarettes—that became my real gateway drugs, far more damaging than the illegal ones had ever been. For years, too many years—they were my escape until the day came when I could no longer escape from them.

In late high school, I experimented with LSD, mushrooms, and ecstasy. By my senior year, I had embraced more of a hippie-ish identity. I'd get picked up in a VW bus after school and head straight to a Grateful Dead show. The price of admission? A miracle and a mushroom. We'd wander through the rows of campers with one finger raised in the air, a universal sign asking for "a miracle." The miracle, of course, was a free ticket to the show. Sometimes, kind souls would take pity on us, offering not just tickets but mushrooms as an alternative gateway.

The scene outside a Dead show was where I felt most alive—a

vibrant, chaotic space where I belonged. Yet, despite the free-spirited lifestyle, I always cleaned up when it mattered, whether for school or a job interview. It was a delicate balance of living on the edge while keeping one foot grounded in the "real" world. Based on what I had witnessed in my family, I was never willing to plant both feet in the Grateful Dead community. I knew deep down that committing was too risky—being a lifelong "druggie" wasn't my destiny.

By the time I turned 21, I was tired—officially in my burnout years—and that's when I got married. I walked away from anything illegal. It had been a short stint of partying with illegal drugs, but trust me, I made the most of it while it lasted.

Once I got married and had kids, my focus shifted. I became consumed with being the perfect mom, wife, employee—you name it, I tried to perfect it. But here's the thing: perfection is bullshit. It doesn't exist. Yet, seeking perfection became my drug of choice. I traded wild nights for two or three beers each evening, nothing illegal, just inherited tradition. After all, I came from a long line of loggers, drinkers, and world-class deniers.

When the time came to face the demons I'd stuffed into the closet for decades, I was 47 years old. I approached it with so much trepidation that it felt like the scariest thing I'd ever done in my very full, very messy life.

In doing so, I realized I had fallen into the very pattern I had vowed to avoid—for years, I had hidden my trauma, my pain, and my emotions. I had buried them deep, so I could raise my kids, pay off the mortgage early, and muscle my way through life. I had convinced myself that, if I could just keep everything tucked away in the backyard of my mind, I could pretend I had mastered life. In reality, those weary bones I'd laid to rest were still aching, still waiting for me to confront what I had tried so hard to ignore. But the cracks in my foundation were impossible to ignore. The weight of being a pretender had settled in my body, my breath, and my bones, until every muscle felt like it was holding up a lie I didn't believe anymore.

Ryan and Roy had shown me firsthand the destruction drugs could cause when used without care, without respect for their power.

For me, the hardest part of using therapeutic psychedelics was silencing the voice of doubt—the voice that echoed society's warnings, branding these substances as dangerous and forbidden. But I had to reconcile that with the possibility that the same "bad" drugs might hold the key to healing the deep wounds I had carried for so long.

This time, the purpose was clear: to bust open that trauma closet, kick down the door, and walk in like Sharly—a total badass. But a different kind of badass. The kind that enters the arena not with armor, but with courage, grit, an open heart, and the willingness to face the broken parts of myself.

By that point, I had nothing to lose and everything to gain. At 47, I felt hollow, like one of those fragile Easter bunny eggs—brittle on the outside, empty within. And I imagine that's how my cousins, my aunt, and my grandma must have felt, too.

I needed to earn my life back—to reclaim something that had been lost deep inside me, and maybe even something lost in all of us.

And though it felt both improbable and impossible, I still held onto the belief that my healing journey could somehow mend the frayed threads of the patchwork quilt that was my family. If I could heal myself—through the purging, the crying, the unearthing of buried pain—then maybe, just maybe, that hard work could ripple outward. Maybe it could heal its way through the tangled webs of addiction, abuse, denial, and destruction.

I have lived with the harsh truth that one person's wounds can ripple outward, wounding not just themselves, but their family, their community, and their lineage. But what if it could work in reverse? What if one person's healing could spark a wave of redemption strong enough to carry legions with it?

During multiple ceremonies, my family was with me in every way. They are my blood, my history, and my roots—and I carried them in my heart and mind as if we were all packed together in a giant, lumbering tuna boat of a car, crammed to the brim with the weight of everything we've been through. I imagined a vessel built from everything we'd survived—no longer held together by pain and duct tape, but fortified with love and redemption, carrying us toward something new.

Together, we would drive off into the sunset, as the horizon glowed with the future, we had always deserved but never thought we could have.

Something brighter.

Something better.

Something finally whole.

"FLOWERS"

Nathaniel Rateliff, Gregory Alan Isakov

CHAPTER 10

TOUGH BROADS, RAINIER BEER

Mothers are our first human connection—a bond forged in a shared life force. The relationship is sacred—whether in presence or in absence. They can be our champion, our guiding light, or the source of wounds that leave us drifting, and untethered. My mother was both.

I remember when she was soft and nurturing. The smell of banana bread in the oven, Halloween costumes spread across the kitchen table, family gatherings where we belonged to something whole. But reminders of normality become a curse when life gets upended. Looking back, the irony stings—the most "normal" time of my life was when I was silently suffering abuse.

She had once been the golden girl of a small town, celebrated at dances, and always picked for the cheer squad. But life had other plans. A college dream ended in trauma. A forced return home led to rushed marriages—two divorces before 23. She longed for escape but ended up trapped, drawn to men who mirrored the very cycles she had hoped to break.

She dreamed of escaping to something bigger—and tried. But her choice in men, her "picker," was tuned to the wrong station. She gravitated toward loggers who drank beer, got into bar fights, and embraced a simple life marked by addiction, living paycheck to paycheck, and clinging to their country roots.

Instead of rewriting her story, she became another woman with crushed dreams—a cigarette snuffed out in an overfilled ashtray.

My mother's wounds didn't start with her. Our lineage was a chain of entangled, fractured relationships. My grandmother, unable to embrace my mother's light, dimmed it at every turn. And behind her was my great-grandmother, a formidable matriarch who carried the weight of 13 children alone after my great-grandfather took his life in the attic.

The women before us were tough because they had to be. They carried burdens no one should bear, passed down like unwanted heirlooms. So, my mother inherited hardship instead of love, and grit instead of softness.

Despite her small stature, my great-grandmother, Mabel, carried an immense presence. She was quiet, always wearing a gentle smile, with a reassuring "hmm" that seemed to say she both understood and was pleased with how the family gravitated around her.

Her house was small. Everything was small—the kitchen, the bedrooms, and the bathroom, somehow, it contained a love far larger than its walls. In the winters, we squeezed together in the cramped dining room, our hands wrapped around coffee cups wherever we could find a place to perch. When the sun was out, we preferred the space beneath the towering trees, lounging in lawn chairs, sipping iced tea, and soaking in the warmth of something much greater than the sum of its parts.

Her tiny white house sat in the middle of Prineville, Oregon, a natural gathering place. Positioned just off Main Street, it offered the perfect vantage point from which to see visitors' cars approaching from all directions, ensuring a constant flow of family and friends.

The house radiated warmth—full of laughter, tears, love, and connection. She carried a timeless grace. Her hair was set weekly at the local beauty salon, and round glasses framed her wise eyes. A pitcher of iced tea was always within reach, a quiet testament to her ever-present hospitality. She favored polka-dot polyester dresses and pearl earrings; her relaxed demeanor exuded the wisdom and ease that only age and experience could bring. With her silver hair and gentle presence, she was the most adorable great granny.

Whenever the small white front door opened, the boisterous greeting was always the same, *Where's everyone at?* Inside and out, the house was alive with activity. At any given time, five to ten people might be gathered—some sipping iced tea in the aluminum chairs outside, others perched on the little red kitchen chairs with a coffee in hand. Kids banged on the piano in the front room, filling the space with chaotic melodies, while others ran through the yard, their laughter carrying on the breeze.

It wasn't just a house; it was a home, in the truest sense.

The men congregated in my uncle's garage, drinking Rainier beer—a sanctuary of tools, conversation, a pool table, and easy camaraderie. Meanwhile, the kids, left to their own devices, would sneak into my uncle's room, giggling over his stash of Playboys, adding a mischievous note to the lively scene.

Madge, my uncle's white bull terrier, patrolled the house with her stocky build and black-ringed eyes, and her no-nonsense demeanor keeping watch over the constant ebb and flow of visitors. My uncle Tex, in his mid-50s, had taken over full-time care of my great grandma. Her house was somewhere we went often, not for any reason but to exist in its slow, steady rhythm. There was an unhurriedness in that house—people wandered in and perched for a while to discuss nothing of importance or the latest town gossip.

She passed away at 99 years old, taking the spirit of the family with her to the grave. The house was sold, and everyone disbanded—scattered like leaves in the wind.

Her daughter, my grandma, carried a thick resilience—the kind forged by a life shaped by a single mother, a deceased father, and 12 siblings. We didn't talk about her father; he didn't exist in anyone's mind. He had given up. The rest of us threw our cards into the pile and saw what life dealt with us.

Because she was beautiful and popular, my mother was my grandma's least favorite child. My grandpa, a quiet man, was unwilling to step in front of a short woman on a warpath. He just let things be—decisions that, as is often the case, carried consequences long after the children left the nest.

My uncle joined the military, proving that sometimes the best way out of a madhouse is through basic training. My aunt took another route, having two children in high school with a man not worth his weight in salt.

After divorcing my father, my mother remarried and settled us all in the Willamette Valley, where she had my brother, Mike. By her third marriage, reality hit—she was suddenly a single mother with no actual job skills beyond being a seamstress for a high-end clothing store. My brother and I would goof around in the car, singing along to "Break My Stride" while Mom ran repaired clothes into the store. She'd collect her payment, and we'd head back home to make dinner—piecing life together one stitch at a time.

After the divorce, my brother, mother and I wandered lost for a decade, unable to find a way back to a sense of home. We moved from one small town to another, Silverton, known for its lush greenery and general lack of things to do. My brother and I started at a new school and quickly made friends with the neighborhood kids on the school bus.

Orla, a friend of mine, lived just around the corner. Her Australian mom's thick accent gave her a unique edge in our small town—an unmistakable presence that made her stand out. But beneath the charm of her voice was a world-class complainer, a certified harper of grievances. At Orla's house, we were a disappointment the moment we stepped over the property line—and, as if that weren't punishment enough, you'd be force-fed Vegemite and Ovaltine as penance.

The neighborhood had its own cast of characters: a brother, a sister, and a guy around the corner. Between us, we were officially the latchkey kid syndicate. It was a working-class neighborhood; during the day, parents were nowhere in sight. We ran that place like a band of outlaws—a vast, forested mountain to explore and no one to tell us otherwise.

It was the ultimate 80s kids' paradise: BMX bikes, pantries to raid, and absolutely no rules—a trifecta guaranteed to lead to stitches, trouble, and stories worthy of a juvenile detention brochure.

We lived in a depressing little duplex; if the walls could talk, they would have sighed deeply and said, "barely scraping by." The furniture situation was minimal at best—think garage sale rejects—and the divorce had left our family in financial shambles, with the ex doing time and us eating *shit on a shingle* almost every night.

For the uninitiated, the gourmet *shit-shingle* recipe featured tuna, milk, and flour slathered on a piece of toast. If it was payday, we got a fancy version with a can of Campbell's mushroom soup and some peas, elevating the dish to our version of fine dining. People whispered that my mom might have developed an eating disorder, and maybe that played a part, but the truth was simpler and sadder: she didn't eat because we couldn't afford it.

A nice religious family lived across the street, but latchkey hooligans like us could rarely mingle with their kids—our level of chaos was listed as a hazard in their parenting manual. Around this time, my mom started dating Darrell, a man in his 30s who had perfected the art of avoiding commitment. With two kids in tow—a 9 and 7-year-old luggage set—my mom might as well have been waving a red flag in his direction.

But Darrell was always game for a *good time,* which, in his world, translated to my brother and me sleeping on his couch while my mom got the bed. I remember thinking I needed a vacation—not from life, but from adult men. I had given them a chance, but they had proven to be duds. His indifference to us was so profound, it could have been mistaken for a groundbreaking meditation technique in some self-help book. Eventually, my mom and Darrell broke up and we moved to Hillsboro, Oregon just outside of Portland.

In Hillsboro, we continued the financial struggle, living on the low-income end of the neighborhood. The kids walked through the park together for safety, a silent understanding that numbers meant protection. One day while walking home, we found a decapitated dog's head near the playground; after that, we took the long way home on sidewalks through neighborhood streets.

We couldn't make rent, so one day, we came home to find the

locks had been changed on the doors, a brutal confirmation of how little stability we had. This was the period during which my brother, overwhelmed by stress and a growing fascination with destruction, started setting everything on fire—small acts of rebellion, maybe, or an attempt to take control of something in a world that kept taking from us.

We were miserable.

My mom tried—she really did. But she was exhausted from raising kids on her own, and she wanted a partner to lighten the load. Instead, the men she chose only added layers of chaos and damage, the kind that would later guarantee enormous therapy bills.

That was when she married Chump. After years of questionable decisions, Olympic-level gaslighting, and enough red flags to decorate a parade route, she finally divorced the dickhead—an overdue upgrade we all celebrated.

I imagine that years of barely scraping by, eviction notices, and impossible choices wore her down, fraying all her edge until the decision to marry him felt less like love and more like survival.

During my mid-teens, and after leaving Chump, my single mother and I had cohabitated—like two pissed-off juveniles trapped under the same roof. My mother reliving her neglected youth, and me consumed with the unbridled rage of a teenager. Our battles were fiery and relentless, fueled by the friction of unmet needs and unresolved wounds.

I made a promise to myself: if she moved in with another man, I would move out. When she started dating again, I kept my word. She bought me a backpack, and we both understood—it was time to move on.

She stayed in town. I stayed in town too, but after I left home, she treated her mid-life crisis like a divine calling—South American adventures, a younger roommate, and a Harley Davidson. One day, I found her pinned under the motorcycle, all 115 pounds of her trapped beneath a machine she had no business riding. She sold it soon after. I rolled my eyes, and we waited for the next reckless decision to land.

I started dating the man who would soon become my husband, Dean. He towered over me at 6 '3", with a clean-cut brownish-black haircut that gave him the air of a classic all-American guy—he could have been the star quarterback in a teen movie, minus the football. For me, he was a novelty. Dean had a wardrobe full of cotton striped polos with a couple of button accents, a style that perfectly balanced his—*I'm relaxed or professional—you decide* vibe.

He was sweet and innocent, yet there was a quiet determination about him—a resolve to escape the poverty that had shaped his childhood. He carried hope like a fragile treasure, cradled in the palm of his hand, and I could see it there, waiting—patient and persistent, just daring to grow. The countless missed school lunches, the result of bounced checks at the elementary cafeteria, that fueled his determination.

Dean drove a Le Car, which was essentially a glorified go-kart pretending to be a real car. I'd make him listen to Seal on repeat, while he retaliated by blasting out Smashing Pumpkins. The Le Car, with its tin-can acoustics, made both genres sound equally tragic. But we treated it like it was the coolest thing on four wheels. One of our favorite pastimes was taking it to the BMX track and jumping it like it was a Huffy bike.

Every time we hit a bump, the car would groan in protest, the suspension threatened to resign entirely. Dean, gripping the wheel with the focus of a stunt driver, would shout, "Hold on!" as if we were in a monster truck rally instead of a glorified miniature jalopy. I'd be holding on for dear life, certain that the thing would fall apart mid-air.

Because Dean was two years older than me and I had been raised by grandmas who puffed long stogies like they were mob bosses, I insisted that Dean buy me Benson & Hedges cigarettes. "Do I *have* to?" he'd groan, reluctantly stepping out of the Le Car, his head nearly brushing the roof of its silver paint job.

It's my brand.

And he always did.

He wore jeans or khakis with button-up shirts while I sported a tie dye, bandanas to pull my hair back, and turquoise jewelry. From an outsider's perspective, we might not have looked like the best match between the height differences and clothing choices. But we knew what others couldn't see at first glance. Beneath the surface differences was a connection that didn't care about fashion or height, it was built on shared laughter, late-night talks about growing up in poverty, and the quiet understanding that we just *fitted*.

We fell in love—the kind only teenagers can conjure. It was rife with immaturity, heartsickness, and emotional torture. My yearbooks bear witness to the chaos, with lines like, "If anyone dicks you around again, you have my number," or, "Sorry about all that stuff with you and Dean. Call me!"

We were on again and off again throughout high school, but no matter how many times we broke up, we couldn't stay away from each other.

Dean was strait-laced, aside from his penchant for the drinking that came with living in a household of recently released teens. He hung out with a crew of similarly strait-laced guys—mostly former Mormons—who rented a duplex near the college. The duplex was functionally disgusting. Beer cans littered every surface, motorcycles were inexplicably parked in the kitchen, a rat had claimed the space above the refrigerator as its home, and the bathroom shower drain, clogged with hair and grit, gave up on sending water to the plumbing below.

At first, our relationship was lovely, but as time passed, we went through spats of youthful rebellion, releasing ourselves from the confines of commitment. Yet even our breaks couldn't keep us apart for long. Dean was one of the first stable guys I dated, and something in me wanted to hold onto that—for the day I might finally become a "normie" myself.

A couple years after leaving Kansas, when I got my first apartment, Dean came to visit one day—and just never left. We'd broken up more times than I could count on all ten fingers and toes in high school, but somehow, we always found our way back to each other. Despite the chaos of our past, we were simply happy, working through the growing pains of transitioning into adulthood.

We stayed in that cozy studio apartment, building a life out of what little we had. We got a dog, eventually bought a starter home, and from that point on, never lived apart again.

In my early 20s, I hit my burnout years—exhausted by the instability of my childhood and craving something solid. When Dean asked me to marry him during a drive to the mall in his Le Car, I said yes without hesitation. No grand gestures, no over-the-top romance— just a simple, certain *yes*. We picked out a ring while running errands, got married by a justice of the peace, and celebrated with a keg and a trampoline at our reception. It was perfect.

And it still is.

We carved out our own definition of family, love, and foundation.

With Dean, for the first time I could remember, I felt at home—a place where I could finally put down roots and let them grow deep. We came from divorced families, and we knew that once we got married, we would prefer to stay that way

In my mid-20s, my mom moved to Hawaii, and I stayed behind. We kept in touch, but she built a life thousands of miles away.

At 26, I stood outside my office, gripping my phone with clammy hands, my gaze fixed on the pavement as I dialed her number.

I was pregnant—terrified, unprepared, and convinced I would ruin a child the way I had been ruined.

For years, I had sworn I would never have children. The thought of it paralyzed me. After everything I had been through, I didn't believe I was worthy of traditional family life. I didn't know how to live it, let alone give it. I was certain I was beyond repair—and the last thing I wanted was for a child to inherit a broken mother.

The phone rang once. Twice. By the third ring, she picked up.

"How are you? Great to hear. Mom, I'm pregnant."

The words tumbled out in a shaky breath. I was an emotional wreck—happily married, and now a college graduate, but still convinced that having kids was a catastrophic mistake. Motherhood had never been in my plans, ever. When the doctor gave me the news, I genuinely tried to convince him I was dying of cancer instead. I was certain he was wrong. Nine pregnancy tests later and a follow-up appointment only confirmed what I had refused to believe. I was in deep, suffocating denial.

She didn't hesitate. "Katie, that's a bummer. You had your whole life ahead of you."

The air left my lungs. That confirmed everything I feared—I was completely and utterly screwed.

She did not mince words. And in that moment, more than anything, I needed my mother—a mother—to tell me it was going to be okay. Instead, silence settled between us, heavy. I felt alone.

That moment ignited a firestorm of anger, frustration, and the quiet sadness that had been buried beneath years of my silence. I had harbored resentment for so long, swallowing it, and keeping my mouth shut. Sure, I had acted out like any teenager would, but she remained in denial—unwilling to acknowledge her role in my childhood wreckage.

Something about her hardness when I needed her support about the pregnancy set off a chain reaction of fury at unaired grievances. It consumed the space in my heart where love should've resided. Her refusal to acknowledge my challenging childhood, paired with her complete lack of accountability for her role, left us in a cruel performance—two actors on a stage: the blind and the silenced.

I carried the weight of her indifference like an anchor. I swallowed my resentment and played the part. It was the "buck up" plan—shut up, push through, and pretend the damage didn't exist. But it did. A slow, simmering resentment stretched between us, an unspoken truth neither of us wanted to face, even though it had unfolded over decades.

Motherhood immediately changed me. The moment my daughter was placed in my arms, everything shifted, as if my life had been leading to this singular, blessed moment.

Up until then, I had been terrified, convinced I wasn't worthy, that I would fail her the way my parents failed me. But as I held her, the doubt melted away, replaced by a clarity I had never known. I saw a future I had never dared to imagine—volunteering at her school, packing lunches, and driving for field trips. A life I once thought was beyond my reach suddenly felt like it had been waiting for me all along.

And I built that future. It became my movement, my purpose, my redemption. Holding her in my arms was proof that I was not broken— that something greater than me saw my worth, my higher purpose.

Seventeen months later, I had my son. This time, I wasn't afraid. I couldn't wait for my future.

My mom sensed this shift, and she started coming to visit every few months to help out or just spend time with them. She wasn't exactly motherly, but she was present. She had deeper conversations with them. My children built a bridge between my mother and I— their love softening the jagged edges of our past.

We chatted daily after the children were born, running through the activities. There was so much life to cover—their adventures, play-groups, friends, our lives were just so beautifully rich.

For years, we continued this path. Eventually, when my kids were in high school, my mom and her husband moved back to the same town where I was raising my family. But it wasn't enough. Healing requires more. After the kids moved out of the house, it was time to focus back on the adults.

For most of that year, I attended psychedelic ceremonies alone, a lonely but necessary journey, one I hoped would bring me closer to the healing I was so desperately yearning for. But as I neared the final stretch, something in me shifted. I no longer wanted to do this alone. My mom was aware of my use of therapeutic psychedelics and was both supportive and curious.

"Mom, what do you think about joining me for a ceremony in a couple of months? Just you and me."

She agreed. Maybe she saw the changes in me. Maybe she wanted to heal, too. Maybe, for the first time, she was willing to meet me in the liminal space where our pain resided.

The ceremony required extensive travel, with MDMA and psilocybin administered under the guidance of a trained facilitator and several assistants. The house held an average of 20 participants, all seeking a breakthrough, a release, or a reckoning. These ceremonies were never recreational; they were sacred spaces for deep healing.

We spent time getting to know the others, then gathered in a circle for the opening discussion. Reverence filled the room as we each set an intention. One by one, people shared their purpose: *I intend to let go of fear. I intend to forgive myself. I intend to open my heart.*

When my turn came, I took a breath and spoke the truth that had been waiting for this moment.

"I intend to spend time with my mother to heal our past wounds."

Five sober facilitators moved throughout the space, quietly checking in, making sure we were okay. But I knew this journey—the one my mother and I were about to take—was ours alone.

It was time to open the door to childhood, the one we had closed behind us.

There is profound liberation in facing the past, taking accountability, and breaking cycles of abuse. I saw, perhaps for the first time, that she needed to face it—not just for herself, but for me—and for the generations that would follow.

Denial had kept her stuck, stunting her emotional growth. Now, it was time to take a walk through our graveyard.

Before the ceremony, we sat alone in a quiet living room. I asked if she wanted to hear the chapter I was writing for this book about Chump. She agreed.

I read aloud, my words filling the space between us. When I finished, she was silent, as if she were processing it. I think hearing the truth spoken out loud was harder than she had expected. Harder than reading it in her own mind. There was no escape from pain when it had a voice.

When the medicine took hold, she got sick. I asked her why—MDMA rarely makes anyone vomit.

"The words. Hearing that story made me disgusted."

I saw her life tree—withered and languishing, teetering on the edge of death in our shared existence. The disease that had taken root in her had spread far deeper than my own, its decay woven through generations.

In ceremonies before this first one with my mom, I had faced difficult truths, peeled them back layer by layer, purged them into buckets, and unraveled them afterwards in integration therapy. I was beginning to emerge with a fragile but growing sense of peace. Her wounds remained untouched, tangled in the weight of unspoken pain. It was clear—her healing had yet to begin.

In the evening, we sat outside by the firepit, nestled on a bed beneath the open sky. The flames flickered against the night, casting shadows that danced as if they were listening.

In whispered tones, I confessed everything—the abuse, the buried stories, the words I had never dared to escape. Years of silence unraveled in the glow of the fire, my darkest secrets spilling into the night, no longer locked inside me but finally set free, carried by the rising embers.

We knew the broad strokes of what had happened, but now there was no escaping the details. She listened the entire night, never turning away. She held me close as we cried, her arms wrapped around me with a tenderness I had longed for my entire life. In hushed tones, she spoke the words I had needed to hear as a child, embodying the maternal energy I had craved but never received.

The medicine stripped us bare—no inhibitions, no filters, and no fear. Together, we sat, staring down at the hungry ghosts of our past, laid the pain between us down like an offering to the fire. And for the first time, we bore witness to the full weight of our shared history, unspoken but never forgotten.

As she held me, she said, "I am so sorry that I didn't protect you. I love you. I wish it were different. I wish I had done better."

A profound reckoning, a necessary healing. We sat together for hours, processed the pain, and unraveled years of silence. And in the end, she said, "I'm sorry." Those two words—all of her words—washed over me, cleansing decades of buried sorrow. I felt seen. I felt heard. I felt loved. And at last, I felt acknowledged.

Honesty reached her heart—it was a blessing, a release. The weight she carried finally had a place to go—away. My healing was not limited to me; it became the lifeline with which to salvage her own.

In turn, I saw her, not just as my mother, but a woman with her own battle scars. She had trudged through life, carrying a monstrous cross on her back. A small-town girl, bright but stifled, trapped in a cycle she couldn't escape. By 23, she was twice divorced, a single mother, being beaten by alcoholic men. The world had hardened her, stolen her softness, and left her with nothing but survival instincts.

Women are expected to hold up the world—sometimes alone—balancing children on one hip and burdens on their backs, moving forward with quiet resilience. We pretend to know what we're doing, never daring to show the weight of it all, never allowed to bend under the crushing load.

And by her early 30s, life had chiseled away her softness. The relentless trials she had endured beat whatever vibrancy or hope she had left out of her heart.

I saw her defeated. That was her life, it had betrayed her, and worn her down until she collapsed under the one job she had once loved—to mother.

And yet, buried beneath the weight, there was a flicker left, a pilot light that refused to go out.

In the end, she did make it right.

And in the end, so did I.

With the sheer will for righteousness that only the wounded could summon, I shattered the cycle of abuse in raising my children. I had no roadmap, and no certainty. But I learned by doing, by being, and by loving.

The abuse, and the tolerance for bullshit—it ended with me. And in its place, I rose—a tough woman, unbroken, standing in my light.

The process of breaking cycles wasn't clean or easy. It was the fiercest battle—against the hidden past, learned behaviors passed down from generation to generation, and unspoken fear. Through that ceremony, we became something more than survivors; we became architects of a new legacy.

To my mother, I simply said, "I know you did the best you could. I forgive you. Maybe you should forgive yourself. These traumas are now our superpowers—if we can survive this, we are powerful beyond all measure."

I meant every word.

In plant medicine ceremonies and spiritual circles, there's often an emphasis on healing the pain of our ancestors. But that's a big ask—a heavy weight, and too much responsibility. But this night with my mom shifted my perspective. We didn't just heal; we redefined resilience—proving that change is possible. We did it for ourselves, for future generations, and for the long line of tough women before us who never got the chance but damn well deserved it.

The truth is, we had never weathered that storm alone. Our ancestors had been in the stands, watching from the heights of time—faces streaked with paint, team colors blazing, and fire burning in their eyes. They had been with us in every moment, willing us forward, daring us to rise. They knew our inherited strength, the power woven into our very being. Our legacy recognized our destiny. They knew our unbreakable spirit—because it endured in them too.

"THE COURSE"
Ayla Nereo

CHAPTER 11

NOT ALL MONSTERS ARE FAMILIAR

I was walking the streets of East Boise, with my backpack swaying as I kicked loose rocks. Dust swirled around my sneakers, as the late afternoon sun beat down on the top of my head. After school, I'd catch a ride to my mom's office, waiting until my shift at the restaurant started. From the age of 13, I'd juggled jobs in the food industry—always working, always moving.

That day, I dragged my feet, dreading the long hours ahead. A blue car passed me in the opposite direction, the driver's face blurred in the sunlit glare. A few blocks later, I noticed it had flipped around.

At first, I didn't think much of it. Coincidences happen. But two minutes later, the car slowed to a crawl beside me. I expected the driver to ask for directions. Instead, leaning out of the window, a man in his late 30s, with brown hair and a round face smiled like an old friend greeting me.

Shielding my eyes from the sun, I waited for him to speak.

"Hey there, you need a ride. I'd be happy to give you one," he said, with a smile that was too warm, almost too casual.

I hesitated. It was only four blocks to the restaurant, but something about his tone set my nerves on edge. His smile lingered a second too long.

"No thanks," I said, forcing politeness into my voice. "I'm almost there."

"You sure?" His gaze locked onto mine, the smile unwavering.

"Yeah, I'm sure. Thanks." My voice was firmer now, and I quickened my pace, moving closer to the row of houses. The car idled for a moment, then turned the corner. I breathed a small sigh of relief.

But two minutes later, it reappeared, creeping along the curb like a predator stalking its prey. My stomach sank. The smile was gone, replaced by an unnerving glare. His hand gripped the steering wheel tightly, his knuckles white.

"Why don't you get in the car?" he said, his tone sharper now, almost a command.

"No," I replied, with my voice wavering, and adrenaline coursing through me. My mind raced, calculating my options. My sneakers were too worn to run, and the houses around me were lifeless, with curtains drawn, and doors closed. No one would hear me scream.

He wiped sweat from his forehead, frustration flickering across his face. "Get in the car," he barked, the command slicing through the stillness of the street.

Panic clawed at me as I walked faster, scanning for someone who could help. The car sped ahead, disappearing around the corner.

My relief was short-lived. One block from the restaurant, he appeared again, his car screeching to a halt. This time, his face twisted with rage. "Get in the fucking car!" he shouted, his voice cracking with anger.

I froze. He controlled the car, the window, and whatever weapon I imagined lurking just out of sight. He had all the power. I pictured a gun appearing any second, pointed at me. My eyes darted to the chain-link fence beside me. I considered climbing it, but I knew I'd be too slow.

Then, as if by divine intervention, a white terrier rounded the corner, wagging its tail. Its owners, a kindly older couple—followed close behind. The woman's soft gray hair shimmered in the sunlight, and the man's weathered face crinkled as he spoke to her. Their presence grounded me, and my panic spilled into a plea.

The woman noticed me first. Her eyes flicked from the man in the car to my terrified face. She leaned closer and whispered, "Do you need help?"

"Yes," I whispered back, my voice trembling.

The driver glared at me one last time before peeling off, tires screaming against the pavement. My knees buckled with relief and fear collided in a wave.

The couple didn't ask many questions. Instead, they wrapped their arms around me, walking me the last block to the restaurant. Their presence was a shield, and their quiet kindness was enough to hold me together. Inside, I fumbled to pick up the phone and call the police, my hands trembling so hard I could barely hold the receiver.

The police couldn't catch him in time, and a few weeks later, I saw his face on the evening news. The details were horrifying: two teenage girls had been assaulted in a park on the East End of Boise. His mugshot stared back at me from the TV screen. His round face and unremarkable brown hair could have belonged to anyone, but it was him. My stomach turned as I thought about the two girls, his victims, and how close I had come to being one of them.

What drove a person to evil? Was it desperation? An insatiable darkness he had carried for years. I pictured a lonely child growing into a broken man, perhaps conditioned by his own monsters. It didn't excuse him, but it added a shadowy complexity to his actions, something that made him more terrifying, not less.

The older couple became a small yet pivotal part of my healing. Their names were Margaret and Frank. Both had retired from their jobs. They checked in on me from time to time, leaving kind notes or stopping by the restaurant to see how I was doing. Their terrier, Pip, wagged his tail happily whenever he saw me, a small reminder that light could pierce even the darkest moments. They never pried and never demanded explanations. Instead, they gave me the gift of quiet, steady support.

That day changed me. I learned that the monsters I'd grown up with—the fathers, stepfathers, and men who haunted my childhood homes—weren't the only ones to fear. Strangers lurked too, waiting, watching, hidden in plain sight in the middle of the afternoon.

But something else shifted too. The experience taught me the power of instinct, the importance of listening to that quiet voice that says, *Run. Fight. Speak.*

Years later, when I walked those same streets, I no longer felt the oppressive weight of fear. I carried something stronger: the memory of survival, the kindness of strangers, and the knowledge that I had the power to protect myself.

I wasn't the same girl anymore. I was stronger, wiser, and unwilling to let the world's monsters steal my light.

"HEAR MY VOICE"
Celeste

CHAPTER 12

$350 AND A BUS TO REDEMPTION

My senior year of high school I found myself with someone who was no good for me—or for himself, for that matter.

Honestly, a blow-up doll would have been a better match—less drama, but the same level of emotional depth.

During my senior year of high school in Boise, he was in his early 20s, exuding a carefree charm that masked a deep unwillingness to face reality. He was all about fun with no concern for the impending weight of adulthood, he lived in a world where consequences didn't seem to exist.

He had a caveman stature: long, wavy hair, a mismatched Bohemian wardrobe, and a face that hinted at Neanderthal ancestry. We traveled to Grateful Dead shows, and chased adventure, but he suffered from Peter Pan syndrome. He was great for spontaneous fun, but deep down, every intuitive part of me was screaming, "Katie, hell no. *Please*, just, no."

I stayed anyway. It was *an adventure*, a lesson in living in the present. However, deep down, I stayed because I didn't believe I deserved anything better.

I spent my life trying to outrun the shadows of my past—years of feeling invisible, unworthy, and desperate to be chosen. The Neanderthal offered the attention I'd craved for so long: wild, carefree, and untethered by expectations. I mistook his recklessness for freedom, and his charm for love. I assumed his chaos could fill the empty spaces inside me.

On Friday afternoons, he'd impulsively travel to a neighboring state to attend a concert, departing within the hour. Hopping from job to job, barely making rent, buying weed with his last ten dollars, or almost burning the house down with a mushroom shaped candle was a typical day. Nothing seemed to concern him about adulthood. If I had fears regarding risky behaviors; he just laughed. I felt his words were a judgment on my rigidity, my inability to relax.

When he moved back to his parents' home in Kansas, I made the questionable decision to sell my Jeepster Commando for a nominal price, just to buy a one-way Greyhound ticket to what would become my personal demise. Kansas was another world—isolated and raw, deep in the woods where his parents owned a shanty town collection of single-wide mobile homes that bore the telltale signs of off-the-grid living born out of desperation.

The property was a patchwork of danger: sweet-natured pit bulls that turned vicious on strays, transient construction workers chasing jobs, and a ravine teeming with Copperhead and Cottonmouth snakes—it was a wilderness that didn't welcome visitors.

A German Shorthair, constantly pacing, lived a confined existence within a large pen. Every time I walked by, I felt an overwhelming grief settle over me. I felt we had a shared understanding that we were both trapped in our own ways. One day, the dog escaped and was hit by a car. *His only way out.*

The entire atmosphere felt thick with unease, and a palpable sense of danger. And yet, there was also a quiet whisper in my gut, a plea to turn around: *Go back to Boise. You sold your car. Quit college. Planning to fail in life. Quitter. All for a boyfriend with no potential.*

I stayed three months, and it was challenging, to say the least. We lived in a beaten-up single-wide trailer with a borrowed dog and a horse that just seemed to loiter in our front yard. I worked at a fast-food joint in a depressing mall, living far too long beneath my life's potential. Each day, I'd hitch a ride into town in a battered Datsun, wearing my fast-food couture, to clock into hell's greasy fire.

Years earlier, I had got a special ring during my time on Saipan— it had a pearl nestled in the center, surrounded by a delicate spiral of small diamonds. That ring meant something to me. It symbolized a beloved place, a cherished past.

When money was tight, and we needed gas and "partying" money, he suggested pawning it. "Katie, I promise," he said, so convincingly I almost believed him. "We'll pawn the ring, I'll work at the construction site, and we'll get it back next week."

But the money never came. His empty promises swallowed that ring, just like my Jeepster, a donation to a lost cause.

For the entire period, I felt like I was tempting fate. Days blurred into nights spent around bonfires with people who never even tried to escape their grim reality. They were born on that land, and from the moment they drew their first breath, it was as if they'd resigned themselves to their fate. Drink. Shoot guns. Chase small thrills that teeter on the edge of danger. And never grow, change or evolve.

His parents lived in a double-wide on the property. When I did laundry, I'd often find his mom passed out on the couch, with a cigarette burned down to the filter in the ashtray beside her. She carried the same chaotic energy as the Neanderthal—drinking, smoking, and being indifferent to the surrounding wreckage. But unlike her son, she wasn't a free bird. A dulling marriage imprisoned her.

His father felt like a predator camouflaged as a nice guy. My childhood had honed my ability to sniff out ill intentions, and I recognized the signs immediately.

"Come give me a hug, Katie," he said, with his voice smooth, and overly friendly demeanor.

As I stepped forward, my chest flattened against his, and a wave of unease crawled over me. His grip lingered just a little too long.

I froze, my instincts screaming, my body registering the warning before my mind could catch up.

His small comments—casual on the surface but laced with veiled insinuations—hinted at something more. Something dark, calculated, and opportunistic.

Here was a 40-year-old man who, given the chance, would have pursued his son's 18-year-old girlfriend without hesitation.

His gaze lingered too long, and his presence carried a weight I couldn't shake—his intentions were unmistakable, unsettling, and all too familiar.

Recklessness hung heavily in that mobile home park, thick like smoke—suffocating, inescapable.

The Neanderthal led the pack of lost spirits, a beacon for those drawn to destruction. He was a novelty, his Peter Pan syndrome both admired and contagious—a man-child who refused to grow up, and in doing so, inspired others to do the same.

People flocked to him like moths to a flame, enchanted by his carelessness, but oblivious to the ruin that always followed.

I wasn't blind. I saw the hopelessness in their eyes, the quiet resignation beneath the laughter. They weren't oblivious. They knew how this story would end—just not how soon.

One night, he invited his male friends and cousins over to the trailer, and in front of a crowd of beer-guzzling onlookers, he suggested we all head to the strip club. I played it cool, accepting the challenge even though my gut screamed otherwise.

We piled into a beat-up car and rattled down the dirt back roads until we arrived at a dismal club. Its flickering neon sign spelled out the promise of sin awaiting inside.

I realized I was the only non-paying female in the room, surrounded by the stale scent of cheap cologne and spilled beer. My boyfriend, basking in the attention of his entourage, announced he was heading to the back "to pick out music" with the strippers. "Katie, Sugar invited me to the backroom. You just stay here, and I'll be back," he casually said,

My stomach churned. I sensed their scheme without needing to follow.

I glanced around the bar—a double-wide mobile home converted into a backwoods male fantasy. The flickering neon sign outside had only been a prelude to reality within: a space that radiated dangerous energy, boundary-crossing vibes, and an unspoken promise of chaos.

Sugar looked at me with veiled disdain, as though I were some innocent, misplaced creature she could outwit with her Kansas-stripper street smarts. Her stringy brown hair hung down on her back, her bedazzled pink bikini dulled by years of wear, and her scuffed black heels looked like they belonged in a discount bin. She was a predator, men were her prey, and I was nothing more than an inconvenient distraction.

This wasn't a place where women's brains mattered—only their skin, and their skill at separating men from their money. The air reeked of desperation, a waiting line of predators eyeing their next move. I was a target, not for their lust, but for their loathing. The dancers saw me as young, as someone who still had a way out, and that made me a threat. They needed to satisfy men to feed their kids. The men, on the other hand, saw me as a challenge—one that wasn't easy bait. That only made the hunt more enticing.

I was in danger, and I knew it.

A heavy atmosphere of sweat, stale smoke, and regret hung in the air. Years of toil and despair had marked each stripper, their eyes and bodies bearing the weight of hard lives. I could feel the unspoken rules of this place; boundaries weren't just blurred—they didn't exist outside the almighty dollar.

Sugar shot me one last glance before disappearing into the backroom with my boyfriend. My stomach twisted into knots. I knew what lay beyond that door without looking; nothing positive was waiting there.

When I protested, "I don't want to wait here alone," his response was a curt, "Too bad."

Two men, fellow partygoers, sat with me. They had also failed to gain entry to the exclusive backroom. We were the leftovers, relegated to the front room, waiting under the dim, flickering lights that cast an unflattering glow over everything.

I sipped my drink, careful not to draw attention to myself. I didn't leave the table, and didn't raise my eyes. Instead, I stared down, feigning deep contemplation as the music pounded and women danced on the makeshift stage—a shaky platform of plywood anchored by a lone stripper pole.

Humiliation and anger simmered just beneath my skin, their heat rising with every passing second. My drink, my stillness, and my downward gaze were all shields against the storm brewing inside me. But as I sat there, the truth became unavoidable: I had reached the end of the loser train.

A faint whistle, barely audible, signaled my stop approaching. That moment brought the realization: my departure. I was at a strip club with a boyfriend who treated me like shit, barely scraping by, flipping burgers instead of going to college. The odds were high that, at that very moment, he was cheating on me in the back room or snorting our grocery money up his nose—or both.

Back at the trailer, I confronted him outside about what had happened in that backwoods bar. That's when his fury erupted. He grabbed me by the neck, lifting me a foot off the ground as if to remind me of my "place." His grip left bruises, but what happened next still baffles me to this day. On the way down, as he lowered me back to the ground, he bit my nose. *He bit my fucking nose!*

When Neanderthal lifted me off the ground, with his hands tightening around my neck, something inside me cracked wide open. By the time my feet hit the dirt again, I knew I couldn't stay. I wouldn't let his chaos swallow me whole. In that moment I didn't just decide to leave Kansas—I declared that I was done living small and accepting less.

Humiliated, confused, and terrified, I stood frozen, trying to process the absurdity of it all as the Neanderthal sped off in his Datsun. Dirt and rocks sprayed in his wake, leaving me standing in stunned silence.

A construction worker, Eric, who lived single-wide across from ours, had witnessed the scene unfold. I had known him for months, our paths crossing in the unspoken camaraderie of firepit gatherings at the mobile home park, sharing beers under the night sky.

Eric approached with an unexpected gentleness, something that caught me off guard.

His flannel shirt, buttoned as if thrown on in a hurry, concealed his lanky frame. In his early 30s, he wore the weight of hard living—the kind that etched lines into skin and settled deep into the bones. His disheveled brown mullet told its own story, a relic of wear and tear, of a man who had seen too much but spoken too little.

Everything had unfolded so quickly that he hadn't had time to react. But I knew he had seen it—standing at a distance, taking it all in, maybe debating whether to step in.

By the time he walked up, I was alone on that dirt road, standing in front of a single-wide trailer, trapped in the aftermath of it all.

He walked up and held me, his arms firm but kind, scanning the area to ensure the coast was clear. The moonlight bathed us in a quiet glow, as though it too was watching, waiting. I sobbed into his shirt, which smelled like tar, sweat, and long days under the sun. None of that mattered in the moment. He retreated slightly, meeting my gaze. He spoke firmly, allowing no dissent.

"Katie, leave tomorrow. You and I both know you're not safe here. This is not your home. Go home. You deserve better, and we both know it."

Without hesitation, he opened my hand and placed a wad of crumpled bills—$350—all his hard-earned money into my palm. His rough fingers lingered just long enough to press the money toward me as though it were a sealed deal. "That's all I have right now, and it isn't much, but I need you to have it."

Eric's hands were rough, calloused from years of construction work, but his touch was gentle, as if he understood what it meant to break and mend. Despite his steady gaze, profound weariness lingered; he carried the weight of numerous hardships. It seemed he was wishing he could change someone else's destiny just once.

Words caught in my throat as I cried big tears that streamed down my face. I mumbled thanks, feeling foolish, agreeing it was time to leave.

Angels come in all forms. Sometimes, they look like a drifter who can't afford to fix his front teeth, and who carries the scent of hard work and exhaustion yet still understands his purpose—to save a lost 18-year-old girl. Every hand that reached out when I needed it most created a shift in my life, one I couldn't fully comprehend at the time.

I had spent so long believing I was unworthy of kindness that accepting it felt unnatural, like a debt I didn't know how to repay. And when I did receive it, a gnawing question always followed: What would it cost me?

Eric pulled me into a firm hug, his flannel shirt rough against my cheek. 'I'll take you to the bus station first thing tomorrow,' he said, his voice steady but laced with urgency, as if he feared I might change my mind. That night, I hid the money beneath the thin mattress on the plywood floor of my barren room. I had once resigned myself to this life, but now I had seen a new perspective. I fell asleep, my tears soaking through the pillow, dreaming of a new beginning.

By morning, the money was gone. The Neanderthal pilfered it under cover of darkness. In my tearful, battered exhaustion, I had missed it all—the subtle turning of the doorknob, the slight lift of the mattress, and the quiet theft of what was never his to take.

When I woke and saw the money was gone, I found him sprawled on the loveseat, sleeping like nothing had happened. 'Where's the money?' I demanded, my voice shaking. My backpack, already packed, sat by the door.

"I don't know what you're talking about," he muttered, opening his eyes.

"I know you took it," I said, my tone firm despite the lump forming in my throat. "I am leaving now. This isn't working. I need to go home."

He didn't move. His indifference felt like a slap, but I knew I needed a different approach. My hand went to my throat, a silent reminder of everything I had endured, everything that had brought me to this moment. "I need that money to leave," I said, with my voice quieter but weighted with resolve.

With a sigh, he reached into the pocket of his ripped shorts and pulled out the crumpled bills, tossing them onto the coffee table as if he was doing me some kind of favor. "There. Take it," he said, his voice dripping with mock generosity.

I didn't hesitate. I grabbed the money and turned toward the door, each step heavy but deliberate. As I walked out, I felt the broken pieces of myself scatter across the floor, but I didn't stop and gather them. I left them behind, knowing I couldn't carry that weight anymore.

The Neanderthal operated under a rigid belief: every person was solely responsible for their own life. In his mind, this absolved him of any accountability for the destruction he left in his wake. The pain he inflicted was not his burden to bear—it belonged to those who suffered it. He ran this rodeo; participation was open to those who could endure. Most stayed on, but I couldn't. Dysfunction, chaos, and a suffocating dimness seeped from every occupied mobile home. Routes differed; the destination remained constant.

On the way to the bus station, Eric, who was usually guarded, let his defenses slip. In a rare moment of vulnerability, he admitted that his upbringing had felt just as suffocating as the run-down trailer park in Kansas. His words carried the weight of years spent under an oppressive roof; a childhood shaped by the same kind of desperation we were both trying to outrun. He'd seen what happened to people who stayed too long, who let the chaos and despair swallow them whole. 'Katie, you remind me of my mother,' he said, his voice low. 'She didn't make it out of marriage with my father. But you can.'

His words lingered in the air between us, heavy with unspoken truths. I could see the ghosts of his past in his eyes—the weight of a childhood spent under the rule of a man who saw kindness as weakness and cruelty as currency. And then, as if fate wanted to drive the point home, I remembered the weekend when I had met his father.

His words had landed like a punch to the gut—casual cruelty spoken with the same ease as discussing the weather. "When a stray dog comes onto my property, shit, I don't even waste money on a bullet. I use a hammer."

He said it with grotesque pride, as if it were a lesson in practicality rather than a confession of brutality.

The darkness of those words settled deep inside me, a dead weight I carried long after I left that house, long after I drove away.

It was more than just a horrific statement—it was a microcosm of my life at the time.

Everywhere I turned, cruelty wore a mask of indifference. Mercy was considered a weakness, survival meant accepting the worst in people, and kindness was a fleeting, fragile thing—easily shattered under the weight of a hammer wielded by human hands.

With the money in hand, I rode the Greyhound home to Boise. The bruises on my neck, the finger indentations, and the bite marks on my nose were just the surface signs of the deeper emotional scars I carried from Kansas.

I'd seen it all on the Greyhounds I rode growing up—humans at their most broken, and beyond. Yet, no matter how fractured or poor we were when we climbed aboard, there was an unspoken solidarity, a quiet agreement to hold space for the one who needed it most. That night, I desperately needed help, and everyone on board knew it.

On that trip, they cared for me—not with words, but through shared glances, quiet gestures of kindness, and an unspoken mutual understanding. Most Greyhound passengers lacked possessions; however, shared experiences unified them. And that small, fragile something was enough. Sufficient escape from Kansas' despair was within reach, and hope beckoned.

The German Shorthairs caged existence still haunts me. In Kansas, I was no different—trapped, restless, waiting for a way out. But unlike that dog, my story didn't end in tragedy. I made it out. And for that, I am grateful.

On reflection, I can see how I confused cruelty with passion, and recklessness with authenticity. I thought I was breaking free, chasing a life of adventure, but all I was doing was running headfirst into someone else's mess, hoping to find myself along the way.

Years later, I saw the Neanderthal at a dive bar, worn down by time. He wore a fedora with a feather, a candy necklace hanging among layers of beads, and his front tooth was missing. He called himself the Gypsy Captain, a title that was more tragic than whimsical.

For a long time, I wondered if he ever regretted what he'd done, if there was a sliver of the man, I had thought I knew buried under the wreckage of who he became. But standing there in that dive bar, I realized there was no mystery to solve. He'd chosen his path—and I was grateful I'd chosen mine.

Seeing him confirmed what I already knew: leaving Kansas wasn't just the best decision I ever made; it was also the one that saved my life. I pondered if he had remorse, wondering if the same person remained beneath the surface.

Kansas was the crucible that forced me to confront myself.

There was so much insidious shame and humiliation tangled up in my life. My healing journey was marked by the shame others inflicted upon me and the darkness of my own decisions. Of all the emotions and endless processing, I've worked through in ceremonies, shame was the most nefarious son-of-a-bitch to rip off.

It was layered, like sediment in rock, pressed down by years of self-betrayal and unkindness. It's insidious because it would creep in daily if I let it—through my habits, the way I treated myself and the choices I made. Drinking too much, gossiping, and settling for a life far below my worth all decorated my existence with the tar of shame. It was the heaviest veil to lift from my soul.

Underneath all the emotional weight, I knew there was a good human. Through every ceremony, I dusted off the shame, layer by layer, like sanding down on an old, battered surface. Over time, the original paint job began to shine through—sparkly and bright, waiting to be seen. Grace saved me. It reminded me that I could reinvent myself and learn to be human again—imperfect, lovable, and deserving of a clean slate.

Every choice I made, every decision to reject the chokehold of shame, was a vote for the person I was becoming. And through grace, I finally understood that shame is a choice, and it's one I'll never make again.

"ME AND THE DEVIL"
Soap&Skin

CHAPTER 13

SUICIDE AND THE COST OF SILENCE

My husband's voice came through the receiver, barely more than a breath. "She's gone."

The words hit like a punch to the ribs, knocking the air from my lungs before my brain could even register them.

Something inside me ruptured. A sound—part scream, part whimper—escaped before I could stop it. It wasn't human. It wasn't me. It was something ancient, something raw, clawing its way from the deepest part of me

My mind refused to accept it. I asked again—once, twice—"What? Are you sure?" My voice cracked, as desperation bled into every syllable.

It didn't make sense. Shana was the strong one—the unshakable farm girl who had run the Boston Marathon, her calves sculpted from miles of trails. She was the one who hosted dinners in a pristine kitchen, and who remembered everyone's birthdays. From the outside, her life was a postcard: two dogs, a stunning new house, a cabin in the woods, and a daughter they adored. The kind of life that belonged to a magazine cover—not one that would end in tragedy.

We were in-laws on paper, but we had grown up together, marrying brothers when we were young. We had 25 years of shared history. In her final years, we weren't particularly close—but that wasn't the point. It was the act itself. The unbearable finality of it.

My husband asked me to call the family, and that's when my body betrayed me. My mind turned to a static, blank, humming void. Names vanished, the people I had celebrated holidays with and exchanged Christmas gifts for years. My fingers gripped my phone too tightly, scrolling through my contacts in frantic loops, as my breath sped up.

Who do I call? What are their names? WHAT ARE THEIR NAMES?!

Twice before, my brain had failed me under the weight of stress—those moments where the mind fractures, splitting like a useless, over-sized walnut.

The first time was when my daughter was sick, and her pediatrician insisted she go to the ER immediately. I had dialed my husband's number 1,000 times before, but at that moment, my mind went blank.

The second was the night I woke to find a man standing in our backyard during a midnight trip to the bathroom. Both times, my thoughts slipped through my fingers like water, leaving me paralyzed.

And with the call, it happened again.

Karen. Our cousin Karen. Her name finally broke through the fog, a faint light piercing heavy mist. With trembling fingers, I dialed.

When she answered, I tried to speak, but the words were fragmented, each syllable too heavy to carry.

"Karen, it's Katie. Shana... it's Shana. She... she's gone."

I whispered the words slowly. They were labored, as if dragging them into the open was physically painful.

I stumbled through the call, but by the time I finished, I was unraveling. *I can't do this.* The weight of it crushed me. I asked her to call the others, with shame washing over me as I surrendered. Failure settled deep in my chest, a cowardice I couldn't shake.

Even as I whispered the words, the truth felt unreal. *Shana. Gunshot. Suicide.* The words clashed, foreign and irreconcilable. Nothing about those words fit together. Nothing about them fit *her*.

Everything changed in an instant, the moment that bullet left the barrel. The world split apart, irrevocably. No more questions, no space for disbelief. Only silence and the crushing certainty of the unthinkable.

The day after her death, I went to work, determined to convince everyone—and maybe even myself—that I was okay. I smiled, nodded, and went through the motions, hoping normality would make it go away.

Do the people who die by suicide see the people on earth suffering? We were scattered like the aftermath of a plane crash, some lost entirely, others wounded beyond repair. Invisible scars. Her absence didn't just linger; it tore through us, reshaping our lives in ways we never could have imagined.

Her choice shattered my sense of knowing anyone at all. If *she* could make that decision, then certainty—about anything or anyone—was an illusion.

That summer unraveled me, each loss snapping another fragile thread tethering me to the earth.

The funeral and my daughter's high school graduation party landed on the same day. A funeral in the morning and a party in the afternoon. Family and friends were already en route, ready to celebrate a milestone we had anticipated for years.

The three weeks leading up to graduation were surreal. My husband was consumed by grief and constant on-call family assistance. The basement flooded that same weekend, adding chaos to devastation. And through it all, we were determined to honor our daughter, through heavy hearts.

I sobbed, as we all did, but beneath the tears was only numbness. I had never felt so hollow. *Just keep breathing. Just get through today.* That was all I could tell myself.

The gymnasium buzzed with excitement—the air was thick with the scent of hairspray and floral corsages, and the squeak of folding chairs against the polished floor. Caps, decorated in glittering letters, bobbed above the sea of families crammed into the bleachers. Laughter, cheers, and the occasional shriek of excitement—joy filled the space like a balloon ready to burst.

I sat among them, dazed.

The speeches blurred into white noise. A relentless roll call of futures.

I stood motionless, scanning the crowd, until I saw my daughter emerging from the double doors. Looking determined, she walked briskly toward me. Without a word, she wrapped her arms around me, holding on tightly.

It was both heartbreaking and a monumental collision of love and resilience, captured in a single photograph. My face was buried in the embrace, turned away from the camera. But my daughter's smile shone forward, red lipstick bright against her blondish-brown hair, framed by her ruby-red graduation robe and cape.

That moment—the embrace—will forever be etched in my memory. The weight of loss. The journey of raising a child into adulthood. The unshakable bond between a mother and daughter. Overcoming the fear of raising a child with my past, to adulthood.

We did it. She did it. I successfully raised a child. We made it one more day.

Hope and heartbreak intertwined, a bittersweet reminder of how far we'd come and all we had endured to get here. The early hours feeding her, dressing her for school, screwing up her first haircut, the early morning drives to school, the college scholarship—every sacrifice led to this moment. A bright future with possibility, set against the shadow of an unexpected suicide.

The season of endings and beginnings blurred together. The heat of summer mirrored the unrest inside me—thick, oppressive, and inescapable. Each day I felt like I was walking through a slow-burning fire, with grief licking at my heels, and questions turning to ash before I could grasp them. Desperate for an anchor, I confided in someone I believed to be a friend, who also happened to be my manager.

I was struggling. I didn't want to choose suicide, but I also didn't know if I wanted to live. I couldn't hack it anymore.

Days later, I asked if she had kept our conversation private, assuming she had.

She hesitated and looked away. That was all it took.

My stomach sank before she even spoke.

She hadn't.

Instead of support, she had gone to the higher-ups. They *graciously* offered to replace me—tacking on the polite caveat that I could stay on for a few months if I wanted to train my replacement.

She had been a friend who sent me late-night texts, who captured photos of my children and framed them as a Mother's Day gift. Someone I trusted.

It was a betrayal. My grief had been weaponized, framed as a liability, a reason to replace me with someone less *emotionally impaired.*

That summer stripped me bare. One loss after another, like waves crashing before I could catch my breath. First, my job—gone. Then, my daughter—packing for college. My sense of identity disintegrated, my foundation crumbling. I wasn't sure who I was without these roles to fill. And beneath it all, grief still loomed, a silent beast waiting for its turn to strike.

When summer ended and my first child left for college, I had expected grief—but not a complete shattering. I was moving through my life as if I was watching someone else living it.

We checked every box; organizers, books, and everything else was ready. But nothing prepared me for the moment I had to walk away from her dorm room.

Tears streamed down my face as we drove out of the crowded parking lot. I couldn't stop staring at her window, silently praying for one last glimpse.

I began to unravel. Each event loosened another thread tethering me to the earth. These were the darkest hours of my life—darker than any night of the soul before. I unraveled behind my sunglasses, barely holding it together. Yet when a neighbor passed by, I'd summon what little composure I had left.

Oh yes, I'm fine. Just fine. Thank you for asking.

The words felt hollow, a fragile mask over the chaos inside me.

So, I drank beers to numb the pain, buried myself in work—any work I could find—overate, and indulged in whatever distractions kept the wolves at bay. I didn't confront a damn thing.

The year hurt in ways I hadn't expected. I had spent years priding myself on being a mother; with one child gone, I sensed the impending doom of my son leaving next. *Who was I without kids to raise? What was my purpose? Who was I? What would my husband and I talk about?*

Countless parents, after sacrificing themselves for years, quietly face the same reckoning. There was an unspoken grief, a silent sorrow we were too afraid to voice. While the world expected us to celebrate, I was devastated.

Grief doesn't only come through death. It sneaks in through endings, and through identities that no longer fit. A child leaving home, an uncertain future, questioning my purpose: it all felt like emptiness. A death in its own way.

And then, there was a loss that left no room for metaphor—suicide, caskets and fading memories.

After the suicide, rage came. My feelings wavered between sadness, guilt, and pure anger. *How the fuck could she do that? Did she have any idea? How selfish, for Christ's sake!* Hard emotions that reeked of bitterness, betrayal, and selfishness—a grievance against the dead that they could no longer dispute.

A loss through suicide leaves a lifetime of unanswered questions. The dead can't explain how it felt in the months, days, or moments before their choice. But their death rattles the living.

The air inside the ceremony space was thick with the scent of burning copal and earth. The soft hum of a distant drum pulsed through my body, grounding me. I wasn't thinking of Shana. Not until she appeared, drifting down from the ceiling, her presence flickering like a candle caught in a draft. She stood before me—motionless and broken. Her body curled inward, as if the weight of her pain had folded her into a shell of her former self.

Her mouth slowly opened.

Hold me. Please hold me.

I audibly cried, loud enough for others to turn and look, as their own journeys were momentarily interrupted by my grief. *"Is she okay?"* they must have wondered.

I saw her—the brokenness in her body, the pleading in her eyes. I held her against my chest like a child. She cried; I cried. I sent her love, finally seeing the fragility that was missed when she walked this earth.

As we exchanged goodbyes, she looked vibrant, and sparkly even. Her purple light fluttered upward. In my mind, I expressed my gratitude, love and support. I watched her drift back into the heavens, waving and smiling as she faded away to nothingness.

Life is a series of choices—some good, and some bad. It would be easy to reduce our lives to the sum of our decisions, but that misses the point.

I didn't want her life to be defined by one choice—one horrible Monday.

She was so much more—a collection of moments, love, and determination. And I, too, had made choices—some good, and some terrible. When people eventually reflect upon my life, I can only hope they see the whole, not just the worst.

The next morning, I questioned whether I had *really* seen her. But it didn't matter. What mattered was the closure, empathy, and understanding of how fortunate I was to have chosen this hard, human life—even in the moments when the weight of it felt unbearable.

Her decision could have been mine at any number of fragile crossroads. I couldn't help but wonder—could *anything* push people back to safe land when they are on the brink of taking their precious life?

I sense her presence—and others who have passed—when they are near. A smile crosses my lips in quiet acknowledgment, seeing, feeling, and hearing them. They linger in the snowflake catching the sunlight, in the warmth of the breeze, and within the hearts of those who loved them. And when joy finally returns after hardship, their favorite meeting place is found in our laughter. If I place my hand over my heart in these moments, a beautiful knowing settles within me. *There you are, I missed you.*

They exist in our moments.

Through the ceremonies, I saw the big life picture.

I am a mother. A wife. A human. A kind soul.

A survivor. Powerful. Connected. Loved.

And now—

I am a woman with a reason to live. Rooted in strength, guided in purpose.

"LIFE AFTER"

Schuyler Fisk

CHAPTER 14

WHEN THE UNIVERSE HOLDS YOUR HAIR BACK

Three months into my year of healing, I boarded a flight to Costa Rica—exhausted, restless, and drowning in the aftershocks of an event that had consumed me. Despite my commitment to change, I remained stuck, my mind looping through every detail, every flaw, and every unfinished task, as if staying busy could keep me from facing the thing that truly needed healing.

By the time I reached the sanctuary in Costa Rica, my mind was still tethered to the chaos I'd left behind—logistics, outcomes, and the endless loop of "what if's." I couldn't see the life-changing journey ahead.

In those early days, I treated ceremonies like they were just another item on my never-ending checklist: *Host the event. Board the flight. Heal.* My mindset was rigid, mechanical, and disconnected. I failed to honor the process or recognize the profound gifts these ceremonies offered. It wasn't until much later that I realized this approach was a glaring reflection of my flailing mental state—always doing but rarely being.

I arrived at a posh resort in Costa Rica known as the go-to retreat center for beginners. Often referred to as "bougie ayahuasca," the resort offers a luxurious, seven-day structured introduction to plant medicine. It's like an elegant boot camp, complete with breathwork, yoga, self-help classes, and integration workshops. By day, there's a packed schedule of activities, and by night, four different ayahuasca ceremonies led by shamans from across Latin America. If there's one thing I've learned, it's that healing—no matter how well-packaged—can be exhausting.

People travel from all over the world to experience these retreats, and that resort is one of the safest places to begin medicine work. With full medical staff and experts in their fields, you have a sense of support. The beauty, the food, and the care—it all came together wonderfully.

During the week I attended, there were about 80 participants, and the ceremonies carried immense energy. This part can be overwhelming, with people purging on mats nearby, rushing to the bathroom, or even vocalizing their experiences aloud. While the music helps drown out some of the noise, earplugs proved invaluable to me. Still, the sounds have a way of creeping in.

Assistants guide some participants outside to process under the night sky, especially those with louder or more intense experiences. I remember a British woman with radiant blonde hair and magnetic confidence, the kind of presence that shifts a room's energy as soon as she steps in. On the third night of the ceremony, her voice rose above the room's cacophony, demanding answers from the universe.

"What the fuck does it all mean? What are you trying to tell me? *WHAT THE FUCK DOES IT ALL MEAN?!*" It was as though she was grabbing the universe by its balls and shaking it, desperate for clarity. By the time the staff guided her outside, she had given voice to the unspoken questions swirling in all of us. What the fuck does this all mean—our lives, our roles, our experiences, and existence itself?

Even outside, her voice carried, as if she were shaking the pockets of life, searching for answers. She articulated what so many of us were too afraid—or perhaps too polite—to say out loud.

At that moment, I realized something profound: if this stunning, self-assured woman—so cognizant of her presence and effect on others—could lose her shit like that, then we all could. With our defenses down, we wrestled with profound uncertainties while seeking understanding.

The next morning, she stood in front of the group, shaken but composed, offering heartfelt apologies for her outburst. She acknowledged both the raw insistence behind her questions and her embarrassment at having lost control. Her vulnerability was palpable.

As she made her way around the group, apologizing in tones full of remorse, I told her to have grace for herself and for the process. It was a moment of mutual understanding—a recognition that we were all in the same boat. We had the potential to lose ourselves in this work, and we all deserved grace.

I realized how I had placed her on a pedestal, perceiving her as somehow better than me in so many ways. Her raw, vulnerable self, laid bare, was a relief. It reminded me that she, too, was a mere mortal, navigating the same messy, unpredictable process of transformation.

Over the course of the night, she found the answers she had been seeking. Though the journey took a toll, there was a glow around her by morning, the kind of radiance that is only earned by walking through the inferno and emerging on the other side, holding life's secret truths cradled in her open hands.

That happens more times than I can count—beauty emerging from the messiness. The questions that haunt us in our darkest hours often seem unbearable, but here's the deal: the freak-outs can be game changers. Sure, they can suck in the moment, but they also have the power to lead people to clarity, purpose, and the answers they were looking for. *Why did we travel so far? Why were folks purging in a foreign land? Why do we drink ayahuasca?* Sometimes, the hardest moments hold the keys to everything.

Then there was the man who arrived with his brother, both embarking on their first-ever ayahuasca experience. They were both fun-natured and lighthearted, though they carried the fiery nerves that come with diving into the unknown.

One brother disappeared into the bathroom, only to emerge in a full toilet paper ensemble: underwear, bracelets, a necklace, and a 16-inch crown. Standing in a Superman pose under the moonlight, he became a ceremony legend.

By morning, as we all gathered to reflect, he approached the shaman with a serious question. He had forgotten the regal TP crown was still on his head; that was the best part. As he spoke with earnest sincerity, the entire group, except for the shaman, tried—and failed—to keep a straight face.

His unintentional humor brought much-needed levity to the room. In a setting often heavy with introspection and emotional release, his playful spirit was a reminder of the joy and humanity woven into the process. We cherished his laughter; it was a precious gift that mended our hearts.

There's a running joke in ceremonies: never trust a fart. I've even heard tales of someone who learned that lesson the hard way.

At one ceremony, a man was compelled to let loose, and through his small cry of "Oh, shit," the entire room understood he meant that literally. You could hear the collective gasp. There's this impression that you won't make it to the bathroom in time, but I've found that most people are aware. Those who heed the warning about trusting a fart emerge unscathed, usually with clean undies.

In ceremonies, conversations bypass small talk and dive straight into the heart of things. There's no time for, or interest in discussing job titles or the roles people play outside their "real" issues. One of the most fascinating aspects of these experiences is the chance to meet the human being behind all the masks.

In our everyday lives, we often follow a predictable script: we exchange hellos, then move to questions like, "What's your name?" and "What do you do?" It feels automatic, almost like we are trained to measure one another by our professional contributions or roles. But in a ceremony, those things are irrelevant. Instead, conversations center on life experiences, the struggles someone is working through, or the pain they're trying to release. Sometimes, people don't even need words; they just need to be held.

By the end of a week, it's common to know the deepest parts of someone, their fears, traumas, and triumphs—without ever learning their first name or what they do for work. And what's beautiful is that none of it matters. There's a kind of freedom in relating to someone as they are, without the filters of titles, possessions, or societal expectations.

In ceremonies, titles don't matter. I've shared space with "big deals," but what matters isn't their status, but their humanity, their struggles, and their courage to face themselves.

In the U.S., it often feels challenging to create this kind of connection in our daily lives. So much of our culture revolves around proving our significance, showcasing our contributions, or highlighting our status. I'm not immune to this; I can fall into it too. But in the ceremony space, all of that falls away. Those who bring their ego or flaunt their achievements find themselves on the outside, as there's little tolerance for such displays. The space demands humility, honesty, and authenticity. Ornate displays of ego don't fly.

Stripped of pretense, I witnessed people at their most vulnerable: broken, exposed, and human. And I witnessed the transformation that honesty, hard work, and sheer grit can bring. It's a primal, unfiltered type of relationship, one that reminds us of the power of genuine connection.

I remember being stuck in my head as we entered the integration circle one morning—a space where people share their experiences after the ceremony. Each person has a time limit, with a bell chiming if they go over ten minutes. Some keep it short and meaningful, while others recite poetry so elaborate you start to wonder if they just love the sound of their own voice.

After hours of being awake, wrestling with my own emotional junk pile, and longing for the sweet relief of a pillow, I often found myself silently pleading for someone to ring the bell on behalf of the collective.

They say there are four types of experiences in an ayahuasca ceremony: body, pinta, consult and nada. The "body" experience focuses on physical responses to the medicine, from shaking to purging. "Pintas" are vision-oriented journeys filled with vivid imagery. "Consult" involves receiving advice or insights from "Grandmother," the spirit of ayahuasca. And then there's "nada"—where nothing seems to happen, you don't recall the night, or in my case, you fall asleep.

"Nada," people say, is a gift—an experience where you rest while the medicine does the work. Over the course of four ceremonies in seven days, I slept through most of them. At first, I was skeptical. How could something so uneventful hold any value? Without dreams or stories to share, it felt impossible to walk away from certain of its impact.

But now, I understand. In her wisdom, Ayahuasca allowed me to sleep through the heavy lifting, sparing me from the full weight of what I wasn't yet ready to face—and for that, I am grateful.

When I arrived at the resort, I was no stranger to nada. I'd spent many ceremonies opting for rest over healing, feeling like I was missing out, while others shared transformative stories. Over time, I worked my way out of that rut, but the fear of missing out lingered.

Stepping into the ceremonies, I carried an unspoken reverence for the shamans, facilitators, and medicine givers. I placed them on a pedestal, imagining them as beings beyond healing, as if they had already grasped the full expanse of the universe. *Were they able to see my struggles? Could they sense the turmoil I carried? Was I more broken than the person lying on the mat beside me? Did my lostness show in my eyes? And, most of all—did they deem me worthy?*

One facilitator met my gaze, his soft brown eyes reflecting my own. In that instant, something in me softened. I wasn't invisible. I wasn't disconnected. In his presence, I felt the weight of shared humanity, the warmth of love, and a glimmer of hope. The medicine givers, the ceremony and kitchen staff were the heart of this retreat. Their care was alchemy that made the space feel sacred.

One night, a shaman and his crew led the ceremony with incredible grace. As they spoke, their words wove a thread between us, reinforcing our connection—not just to each other, but with something much greater. "We are all one." They had brought ayahuasca out of the jungle because they had seen the world struggling. They wanted to help. To guide Earth and its people toward awareness, connection, and change. Their message landed deep within me. This medicine had traveled far, answering a call to heal a wounded world.

As the shaman passed me the cup, his gaze met mine. "Thank you so much," he said. The words reached me in a way I hadn't expected. I was the one receiving, yet he was offering gratitude. In that moment, I saw him not as a pedestal-bound figure but as a human, offering something sacred from his hands to mine. Despite the nervous knot in my stomach, I accepted the cup with reverence, my heart swelling with appreciation.

I lifted the vessel to my lips and drank. The yoga instructor had advised us to "consume it—with intention," but the truth was, I just wanted to get it down. I swallowed it fast, trying not to gag, hoping that, somewhere within this hurried gulp, the medicine would still find its way to me.

What followed was a long, silent night. I stayed awake for most of the 15 hours, yet nothing extraordinary happened. No visions, no profound insights, no emotional breakthroughs, just a restless, unfocused mind. When I went back for the second cup, an assistant asked if I had experienced visions, purged, or received a "consult" from the medicine. I didn't. It was as if the night itself was waiting for me to do the heavy lifting, but I still wasn't quite ready.

On the last night of the ceremony, I approached the shaman and confessed, "I've had three nights of nada." My intention for the evening was simple yet profound: to release behaviors and emotions that no longer served me. That night was different—magical, even—as I watched the shaman standing at the front of the room. He wore a dazzling beaded necklace paired with sweatpants and a t-shirt, an unassuming mix of the sacred and the normal. Yet, beneath the casual attire, his presence radiated deep wisdom and reverence.

That night, I earned the dubious honor of being the first fallen soldier, the inaugural passenger on the barf train. When you first purge, you know you're setting the tone for the room. The sound of retching becomes a domino effect, a reminder that everyone's stomach has its limits.

The vomiting and retching elicit a universal reaction—even the most hardened souls can't help but wince with a sympathetic *ohhh, that was a doozy, poor guy* expression. It's a collective *we understand your* vibe, because everyone ends up holding their own hair back. Just give them a minute.

However, I wised up and started wearing a headband around my neck, ready to deploy it when needed. There's nothing worse than having ayahuasca stuck in your hair for the long trip back to Earth. Pro tip: a little preparation goes a long way.

For me, purging comes with a bonus feature, courtesy of having two kids: a little pee. Not a full flood, but just enough to make it count. This, of course, required a call for the "soul train" golf cart to whisk me back to my room for fresh underwear.

As I made my way back, I rehearsed the next morning's conversation with my mattress mates, determined to clarify: "I wet my plants, not my pants." Making that distinction was imperative—because, let's be honest, nobody wants their spiritual journey overshadowed by the rumor that someone shit the bed when it's not true.

Since then, I've started wearing pads during ceremonies and haven't had a single mishap, which leads me to believe it was all in my head. And if someone ever claims they shit themselves during the night?

Well, it's taken with a grain of salt. After all, in these spaces, embracing a judgment-free process is part of the healing—and sometimes that includes bodily functions.

Purging is one of the most critical components of letting go of all the shit—literally and figuratively. The vomiting, yawning, weeping, laughing, even shitting, are what turn many people off ayahuasca altogether. But avoiding it is missing the point. I spent some of my most profound moments staring into a bucket, asking it what it represented. And, as strange as it sounds, the bucket would answer: "Control, worry, and self-doubt." The list of released maladies went on and on.

At first, I was in the "hell no" camp about vomiting. But over time, I realized the bucket wasn't just a vessel for my stomach's contents— it held all my darkest worries, my fears, and my baggage. The medicine gave me the graceful gift of letting them go. Each purge was like an offering to the bucket gods, a surrender of the things that no longer served me.

Through this process, I understood that control had never been mine to begin with, it was always up to the universe. Most of the things I worried about had never even come to pass, nor had they ever intended to. And my self-doubt? I'd clung to it for so long and so hard that the universe itself appeared to be begging me to give it a break. Release was paramount; it was a purple liquid transformation.

The bucket's response was everything. Hearing what it had to say, what my body needed to release—was a turning point. After the ceremony, I realized that the weight of those maladies had eased. They hadn't disappeared, but they no longer consumed me. What had once felt overwhelming was now manageable, as if the medicine had softened the edges and given me space to begin finding peace.

I discovered a way to keep the purging at bay for at least 30 minutes, giving the medicine enough time to work its magic. As soon as I drank the first cup, I leaped to my seat, rinsed my mouth with water, and spat the contents into the bucket. Then, I chewed a piece of gum for about 20 seconds before wrapping it in a napkin. It wasn't glamorous, but it worked.

The bucket doesn't just receive; it also transforms. Every worry and fear purged into it becomes compost for something new—a flower, a tree, or perhaps just the space to breathe a little lighter.

Over the course of the week, I set three intentions: show me who I have become, heal my heart, and merge me with my soul at all costs. That last one intimidated me, inviting a storm I wasn't sure I could weather.

On the last night of the ceremony, the shamans moved through the room, performing healings on each of us while we were under the medicine. Even though I drank three cups that night, I purged almost immediately, leaving the effects minimal. I seemed sober.

But as the shaman performed the healings, I noticed energy waves rolling off him—rippling through the air like invisible currents. I had experienced no visuals all night, but this was different. It was real. I knew at that moment I had landed somewhere beyond the ordinary—a different place, a different time. There was spiritual magic in the air that night, and it was undeniable.

During my healing, I saw younger versions of myself. It was as though something outside of me—a maternal, nurturing presence—was wrapping me in a hug. Two tears fell from my eyes, drifting down my cheeks, merging at my neck, and traveling together into my heart. It seemed symbolic, as though my heart was healing, and the tears represented the merging of my soul.

The experience was symbolic in so many ways. I arrived as a hot mess, yet I imagine I got everything I could from it. The resort held me, offering a structured environment that helped push me forward in significant ways.

Despite my gratitude for the experience and the sanctuary it provided, a truth settled within me—I needed to go further. I had to step beyond curated spaces and journey closer to the source of the medicine itself.

There's always a certain fear when I head back into the "real world" after leaving a ceremony. This time, I left the space a little more aware than when I had arrived. At the airport, I noticed the peculiarities of the world I was returning to. People were drinking at the bar at 9 a.m.—because, after all, they were on vacation. I paid far too much for some uninspired airport food. I recognized the irony: in our society, people drinking alcohol at 9 a.m. is more socially acceptable than drinking ayahuasca. Most times, the ayahuasca helps people realize that drinking at 9 a.m. isn't all that appealing.

Once on the plane, I couldn't help but observe the woman next to me. She devoured an entire large bag of chips in one sitting, asked for a second helping of pretzels, binge-watched *The Bachelor*, ordered as much alcohol as the flight attendants would serve, and then passed out. I realized how behaviors like hers are normally celebrated—while psychedelics, which offer profound healing, remain taboo in so many circles. The contrast was glaring, and it left me pondering how upside-down our societal norms are.

I tried to lean my chair back, as the man behind me shoved his knees forward, forcing it upright. His tantrum didn't go unnoticed—his wife, exasperated, reprimanded him in audible hushed tones. "Knock it off," she whispered, as she also wrangled their kids. I relinquished the battle, not opting for a fistfight after just leaving the jungle.

At the retreat, they'd encouraged us to examine the things that arise in moments like this. *How does this make me feel? How often do I feel this way in everyday life? Where did I first feel this emotion in my life?* With those questions in mind, I turned my attention to the woman beside me, now slumped over in a stupor. I was annoyed at first, maybe even disgusted—not just with her, but with myself. I recognize this sensation every time I've over-eaten or indulged. Memories of shoveling cookie dough into my mouth without a second thought flooded in. It's self-abuse, a way to numb pain. I've hidden behind my weight for years, treating it like armor. Rolls of flesh were a shield I believed could encase me in safety.

And then I traced it back—back to my stepdad, Chump, and the locked-up Oreos. Food had become my silent rebellion, consumed by anger, bitterness, and frustration. For years, it had been my drug of choice.

I looked at the woman again, now sleeping through her bender of chips and alcohol, and I saw myself. My annoyance and disgust shifted. A well of deep sadness opened—for her, for me, and for the ways we'd both hidden from the things we were unwilling to face. I wondered, *what are we both avoiding? What's lurking beneath the surface? What are we truly ingesting?*

That anger and frustration melted into compassion—compassion for her, for me, and for the inner children we'd both neglected and numbed. In that moment, I sensed the undeniable truth of our shared humanity. I could no longer unsee the fragility, the pain, and the hope in myself, in her, and in everyone else.

And with that understanding came the inevitable questions: *How did we get so lost? Can we find our way back? Why do we accept a world where self-abuse is more tolerable than self-love? How did numbing ourselves become easier than experiencing, and when did we decide that surviving mattered more than thriving?*

These questions weren't just abstract; they were urgent against the edges of my heart, demanding answers, not just for me, but for all of us.

As I stepped back into the world, I realized the greatest gift of this journey wasn't just healing myself, it was the ability to see humanity differently. Through the messiness of ceremonies, I had learned that true transformation requires grace: for ourselves, for others, and for the collective chaos we're trying to untangle. It's not about perfection; it's about showing up and daring to believe we can change.

"BACK TO YOU"
LIVE SESSION WITH STRING QUARTET
Benjamin Gordon

CHAPTER 15

ANGELS AMONG US

As I immersed myself in the soul recovery work, I began to understand how fleeting interactions often hold the key to life's larger moments. In the smallest gestures, people saved me. Over time, the helpers along the way became more than bystanders—they were transformed into larger-than-life characters, my healers. Their compassion rippled through my life, leaving an imprint so deep that I resolved to carry it forward—to be for others what they had been for me. Every quiet moment of grace, and every act of kindness had shaped the person I was becoming.

After my childhood friend Allen died, I felt his presence most vividly in the stillness of night, especially when brushing my teeth. I would speak to the void, with my voice low and trembling: "I'm sorry things turned out the way they did. That I failed you. I couldn't even save myself back then. But I will always love you for what you did for me."

Allen's courage hadn't just been a fleeting moment in my life; our friendship had been a defining chapter. His bravery had planted a

seed of hope within me, one that later blossomed during the transformative ceremonies where I confronted the shadows of my past. I
owed it to him—and to myself—to make it right, and to honor his
sacrifice by creating a life worthy of the faith he placed in me.

There were others, too. Bill, my next-door neighbor, radiated a
life-affirming confidence and joy that showed up precisely when I
needed it most. Marla, with her sharp wit and refusal to take life
too seriously, showed me how to find laughter even in the hardest
moments. Eric, who handed me $350 for a bus ride, and the Grey-
hound passengers—strangers with threadbare pockets—who pooled
their last dollars to buy me water.

These weren't grand gestures, but quiet, ordinary acts of kindness—a mosaic of love and compassion that, piece by piece, altered
my course. They were the hands that steadied me, the proof that,
even in my darkest moments, I was never truly alone.

By the time I had participated in more than ten ceremonies, I
felt like I had undergone countless rebirths. Each one had left me in
a different state, sometimes elated and liberated, other times weepy,
hyper-aware, or lost. While I trusted my ability to claw my way back
to stability, the process was grueling—I knew it was something I
couldn't, and shouldn't, face alone.

Thank goodness for my family and close friends, both here and
beyond. They held me when I cried, kept vigil through the darkest
hours, and stood by me with unwavering support until I found my
way back to myself. Even my dog let me sob into her fur, licking my
hand as if to say, *I'm here—you're not alone.*

After my first few ceremonies, re-entering 'normal' existence felt
like navigating a foreign world. While others measured their weekends
in loads of laundry or garden chores, I measured mine in emotional

weight lifted and traumas released. The disconnect often left me feeling stranded, surrounded by the vast waters of solitude and unshared experiences.

When a neighbor asked about my weekend, I wasn't about to say, "Oh, you know, Frank, just spent two hours vomiting into a bucket, purging years of stepdad-induced trauma. On the plus side, I lost five pounds and evicted that SOB from my psyche." Or "Connie, picture this—I'm on mushrooms, stuck in a deep concrete well filled with putrid alcohol. So, I grabbed an imaginary sledgehammer and smashed it to bits. Emotional concrete is a real motherfucker," I'd say, wiping my brow with mock exhaustion. Instead, I just smiled and said, "It was productive."

As the year ended, I reflected on the overwhelming gratitude I felt—for the survival, the resilience, and the kindness that had carried me through. Each hardship, each act of love, left its mark like layers in stone—pressed into the foundation of who I am, building strength with every passage of time.

When I gave birth to my first child, before holding her in my exhausted arms for the first time, she became everything I had been searching for without even knowing it. Seventeen months later, I welcomed my son, and together, they nestled into the deepest parts of my heart. Their beating hearts gave me the strength to keep going— sustaining me through years I might not have survived otherwise. I was their mother, and through them, I found a reason to live.

My husband is my past, my present, my future, and my forever. Time and again, he has pulled me from the wreckage, offering a life filled with love, a home, and unwavering support. His quiet trust gave me the safety I needed to dive into the depths of my healing, even though he chose not to partake himself. He never questioned my decisions, trusting instead that I knew what I needed.

It wasn't until I worked with therapeutic psychedelics that I truly understood the depth of what my husband had given me. In those moments of clarity, I saw that his love, and his presence, had always been there, constant and unyielding. Trauma had blinded me, but clearing the fog allowed me to finally *see* the beauty of my life.

One night, during a facilitator-led ceremony by a crackling fireplace, wrapped in a white blanket and under the influence of an empathogen and a psychedelic, a voice caught my attention. It felt as though it came from somewhere far beyond my limited mind. I knew it wasn't my voice—how could it be? I had never spoken to myself with such kindness. In soft, rhythmic tones, it repeated: *"You are worthy. You are loved. We believe in you."*

For an hour, the words washed over me in a steady, unwavering pattern, as though some higher power knew I needed to hear them, over and over, until I finally began to believe. A warmth surrounded me, so unfamiliar that I questioned it: *What is this feeling? Why do I feel so good?*

It was as if a stranger had appeared—unfamiliar yet undeniable. Then it hit me: *This is joy.* For the first time, I felt it encase my body, wrapping me in a warmth I had never known before.

A friend sat vigil by my side, her reddish-blonde hair glowing in the firelight. She looked into my eyes and asked softly, "Are you doing, okay? What do you need?" Her love radiated toward me, and I felt it washing over me like a tide.

Without hesitation, I replied, "Someone just convinced me that I'm worthy, loved, and believed in. I don't know who it was, but they really wanted me to understand."

I paused, then added sheepishly, "Maybe water?"

Her response was swift, deliberate—like a pit crew in action. She handed me my water bottle, pushed the straw toward my lips, and looked me directly in the eye. "You're not done yet," she said with quiet conviction. "Go back to that place and listen to them again."

Her words carried a weight I couldn't ignore. I nodded, allowing myself to return to that sacred space. She thus became one of the many guides who gently redirected the course of my life.

That night, I felt joy for the first time I could remember. Now that I knew what it felt like, I realized I could find my way back to it. And I did—time and time again in my sober waking hours. *I felt joy.*

The gift of that night was a seed planted deep within me. It was a seed of hope, belief, and worthiness that would flourish if I nurtured it. *I am worthy. I am loved. Someone—or something—believes in me.*

That night, I saw the angels in my life for whom they truly were, fire-bearers of love who had valued me long before I ever valued myself. Their big and small acts of kindness, rooted in their belief in me, had lit the way forward.

A universal truth settled in my heart as I lay under a blanket by the fire: *We are all worthy. We are all loved. We all have a team—seen or unseen—that believes in us. And they are waiting, with bated breath, for us to believe it too.*

"THIS LOVE"

David Onka, Reels Choir

CHAPTER 16

THE ART OF REMEMBERING WHO WE ARE

The first time I entered a ceremony space; I wondered who else would show up for a psychedelic journey. I thought people would roll up in a VW bus, with the Grateful Dead playing on a crackling old radio, and the scent of patchouli thick in the air. I half-expected a crowd of wandering free spirits, draped in tie-dye and lost in the cosmos to walk through the door.

What I found was far more surprising—a reflection of humanity, in all its complexity.

They were everyday people, navigating life just like me. Veterans, doctors, police officers, entrepreneurs, parents, survivors, seekers— humans in all their many forms. Some carried visible burdens; others masked them well. But once the ceremony began, labels fell away.

Occasionally, a big ego would saunter in as though they owned the place—someone clinging to their self-importance, their achievements hanging off them like thick gold chains, as if life were a never-ending battle for dominance. But oversized egos didn't mix well here. Nothing built walls faster than an ego that refused to take a seat. It repelled real relationships, suffocated true connection, and blinded people to the fact that life isn't a competition, it's a group project.

The people who cracked themselves open, confronted their unchecked behaviors, and chose humility over self-importance were the norm. Because, in the end, we were humans—equally flawed, equally searching, equally fragile. It didn't matter what job people held, where they came from, or how much money was sitting in their bank account.

What mattered was how they moved through the world—the way they treated themselves and showed up for the people they loved. At the core of it, were they a good person, or at the very least, trying like hell to be one?

Outside the ceremony space, the world operates differently.

Tribalism is everywhere—in my community, my country, the world, and sometimes even within myself. The "us vs. them" mentality seeps into conversations, infecting everything from politics to agriculture, the pandemic to global crises. As the year unfolded, I realized it was no longer just about opinions—it became identity, entrenchment, and division disguised as belonging.

Stepping outside my echo chamber came from a deep curiosity about human nature. I wanted the stories—the raw, unfiltered truth of people's lives. I wanted to know where they had been, how they were feeling, and what made them tick as they moved through the world. Through childhood I learned survival mechanisms—adaptability, observance, and respect for the diverse nature of human beings. I engaged with perspectives that I might disagree with, even when it was challenging, uncomfortable, or infuriating.

After the ceremonies, as I stepped back into everyday life, I couldn't help but wonder—what did God, the universe, or any higher power really think of all this division? Would the divine truly care about the battles we waged in comment sections, the endless fights over political labels, affiliations, and ideologies? Did any of it matter beyond the fragile, fleeting constructs we built to separate ourselves?

Did we really believe that love and respect should be rationed out based on which side of an imaginary line someone stood?

Before the year began, I made a conscious choice to push myself—to step beyond my comfort zone and break free from the safety of my personal silo. I didn't want to simply exist in familiar spaces; I wanted to grow. That mindset had already been present in small ways before the ceremonies—I found I was challenging myself at work, in relationships, and in conversations with people who held vastly different beliefs from my own.

But after attending multiple ceremonies with therapeutic psychedelics, I realized something profound: others had already been doing this all along. These spaces were a true tapestry of humanity, woven together by people from every background, culture, and perspective, bringing their own experiences, their own truths, their own pieces of the puzzle. And suddenly, the world felt even more beautiful—not just in its glorious diversity, but in the common threads that bind human beings navigating this life together.

In ceremony spaces, people meet in the radical center—stripped of titles, ideologies, and belief systems. We are simply human beings—flawed, searching, and deeply interconnected. The external pressures fall away—politics, divisions, and the carefully constructed masks we wear. In this space, we see each other for who we truly are, not for the beliefs we hold. We challenge our perspectives, our assumptions, and the walls we've built to keep others out.

We were all different, but cut from the same cloth—struggling, searching, and clinging to the familiar even when it hurt. Some of us found a way out. Others remained lost in the loops or the stories. And all I could do was honor my own path while holding vigil for theirs.

At times, I felt drowned in news headlines, overwhelmed by the endless cycle of bad news, and feeling anger as an unexpected, constant companion in the chaos. Throughout the year, I became aware of my complaining, feeling sad or just venting about world affairs. As if the noise itself was a refuge.

But beneath all of it, I recognized a deeper truth—there was despair behind it. A quiet, unspoken sense of being unmoored. It was disguised as outrage, but I couldn't escape the feeling that lingered below the collective surface keeping us all stuck in the bog of desolation.

More importantly, after a year of ceremonies, I came to a sobering realization—I had missed the point of life entirely. How often had I or all of us—become more invested in fighting the world than in living in it? Drowning in outrage, clinging to conflict, mistaking resistance for purpose—while forgetting that joy, connection, and presence are just as vital to existence. At one point, I, too, had given my power, time, and energy to the negative stories, letting them consume me. But I decided: if I had the chance to wake up to another day, I would choose differently. I would embrace the simple, profound gifts of life—growing food in my garden, loving the people around me, and finding beauty in every single soul I encountered.

Perhaps the most unexpected gift of this journey wasn't just the healing—it was the people. The friendships forged—when a stranger offered to walk beside me, steady and unwavering, an arm around my back as I navigated life's winding trail. These were the relationships that reminded me of something profound: healing was never meant to be done alone. It takes a team.

One night at an MDMA and psilocybin ceremony, a woman in her 90s sat among us, with her frail hands resting in her lap, and her eyes holding decades of stories. She had come to the ceremony with a purpose—not for healing in the way most of us sought, but to make peace with dying.

She confessed to the group, her voice steady but vulnerable, that she knew she was at the end of her life and wanted to meet death without fear. The weight of her words settled over us like a heavy but sacred hush. We checked in on her throughout the night, drawn to her like children to a grandmother, feeling the quiet enormity of what she was facing. It was the same thing that, inevitably, we would all face.

At the end of the evening, I watched as she struggled to steady herself, the mats beneath her feet an uneven terrain. Without hesitation, I crossed the room and offered her my arm. As we walked, she turned to me, her voice trembling with something deeper than just exhaustion.

"I'm so embarrassed that I have to rely on others," she whispered. *"I've always been so independent."*

Her words hit me like a stone in my chest. I felt tears stinging my eyes, not out of pity, but because to me, this was an offering—a rare and profound act of service.

I looked at her softly. "When we help you, it's an act of love. Sometimes in this life, we don't always get the chance to offer that. So, if you can, just let us help you. Just receive the love."

She nodded, her grip tightening around my arm. At that moment, something shifted.

The next morning, she stood before the group, her face luminous in a way that was almost otherworldly.

"I found the peace I was looking for," she said simply.

And we felt the gravity of that peace, draped across the room like a quiet benediction. It settled over each of us, a gift not just for her, but for all of us lucky enough to witness it.

The people I met in the ceremony space were so beautifully different in all of life's complexities. With some ceremony participants, they came to address their illness—cancer, emphysema, incurable diseases—the list was long. It redefined any familiarity or expectation of future days. The personal timeline was a storm of black-and-white static on an old television set—a dull hum filling the silence like a ghost of lost transmission to reality.

How do you find peace when your days are numbered? What if you want to live even after a grim prognosis? How does someone face fear with courage? What are the answers to life's questions that aren't listed in a doctor's chart notes? How do you knowingly leave your family behind? What if giving up hope is defeat?

At a ceremony with 20 participants where MDMA was offered, I had the chance to speak with a man in his late 50s. His bald head bore the mark of cancer's toll, and his body was frail—a shadow of the life he had once lived. Yet his spirit burned with defiance. Beside him, his partner sat vigil, their silent presence a tether to the life he refused to surrender.

At the start of the ceremony, he greeted his illness like a warrior at the gates of battle—unyielding, unwilling to make peace with what was coming. There was no surrender, no soft acceptance, only the fight ahead. "Taxes still have to be done, and business affairs put in order," he said, as if keeping busy could bar the inevitable.

But by the morning, something had shifted. The battle stance faltered. In its place came a quiet defeat—not in weakness, but in revelation.

All we have is this one precious moment—fleeting, irreplaceable, now. And the only question that truly matters is: Do we even notice it? Would I be at peace if tomorrow never came—if this was my last conversation, my last month to live, and my last chance to hold the person I loved for a lifetime?

At another ceremony, a woman revealed she had been diagnosed with Stage 4 cancer, a prognosis that should have provided a death sentence. But she chose to meet her illness head-on, combining conventional medicine with chemotherapy while also turning to therapeutic psychedelics, not just to heal, but to understand what the illness had come to teach her.

Within a year, she was in remission.

A few years later, I sat in at the ceremony with her. By then, her battle with cancer had become a chapter in her past, but the journey had left its mark. Through it all, her partner and her dog had been her rocks, holding her steady as she walked the razor's edge of survival.

Her dog was more than a companion—it was the heart outside of her body. Through the worst of it, the sickness, the uncertainty, the deep unraveling of what it meant to face mortality—that dog never left her side.

Then, in a cruel twist of fate, after she recovered, her dog got cancer.

Maybe it was a coincidence. Maybe it was the most profound act of love—a soul bond so deep that, in the end, the dog took on her illness, carrying it so she wouldn't have to anymore.

In Costa Rica, at an ayahuasca ceremony, I noticed a woman in her mid-40s slowly walking by me. She had shoulder-length curly hair, which framed a face that might have once radiated warmth. She looked like a typical mother type, someone you'd expect to see cheering from the sidelines at a soccer game, packing school lunches, or flipping through the pages of a well-worn parenting book.

But while the rest of us had learned to hide our brokenness, she couldn't. The energy of devastation rolled off her in waves. She had arrived shattered. Days later, I spoke with her. Her name was Susan.

A month before she had arrived at the ceremony, her 13-year-old daughter had died by suicide.

Susan had been a high school principal, a specialist in suicide prevention—a woman who had dedicated her life to saving teenagers blamed herself for missing the signs in her own home. The guilt gnawed at her, replaying the never-ending what-ifs. She left the job she had once loved; she no longer felt qualified to lead others when she couldn't save her own child. Through that, she was searching for a single piece of sanity in the wreckage of loss.

The day we left the ceremony and flew back home, I saw her across the courtyard, smiling and conversing with people. It seemed like progress—a small seed of hope.

In Colombia, I met a battle-hardened female veteran—a dedicated soldier carrying the weight of every war she had served. For years, she had given herself fully to the mission, carrying out orders, witnessing loss, pain, and suffering in ways that most of us could never comprehend. But war had left its mark, and, when she had retired from the military a year earlier, she had carried the weight of it with her.

The stories stayed, woven into her body like old scars, playing on repeat in the quiet moments. So, she set out on a different kind of mission.

For six months, she traveled through South America, sitting in ayahuasca ceremonies, learning from shamans, and walking a path that had nothing to do with war—but everything to do with survival.

I connected with her instantly, and we stayed in touch. She was so damn strong—not just in the way soldiers are, but in the way of someone who had faced the darkest parts of themselves and refused to look away.

Eventually, she sold everything and moved to South America full-time to train under a shaman. She brought with her the same discipline, grit, and fortitude that she had taken into battle—but this time, it wasn't about war. It was about liberation.

She was one of the most peaceful, radiant souls I ever encountered on this path. She was bubbly, joyful, exuding happiness in a way that felt almost divine. She had walked through hell, and, somehow, she had come out the other side glowing.

These stories are everywhere in everyday life, living within the neighbors we pass, and the strangers we overlook. They belong to everyday heroes, the ones who keep moving forward despite the weight they carry. Their stories whispered to me in moments of doubt, quiet reminders that life is a relentless ride—full of highs, lows, and the spaces in between that shape us.

Before the year began, it was easy to get lost in my own story—to let trauma and old wounds play on a loop, trapping me in a past that felt impossible to escape. That was the natural thing to do. The harder thing—the closest to bravery—was to step back, and to truly see. To witness the world beyond my own pain. To understand that suffering isn't a solitary experience, and that resilience is embedded in the hearts of every person I pass. Behind every door, beneath every surface, there is a quiet struggle. And in that knowing, I was never truly alone.

Walking through my own neighborhood, I see it now. We move through the world unaware of the battles others' fight—the strength it takes just to wake up, to push through, and to put on a brave face and step into the day.

But the people I met left an indelible mark on me. I remember their stories, their fortitude, their raw honesty, and their relentless courage. Through them, I became more compassionate, less judgmental, more open to loving a stranger than I had ever thought possible. And in doing so, I learned to extend that same grace to myself.

In the end, I found love—and it found me. Not just in one person or one place, but in humanity itself. The world became my community, and even if they didn't know it yet, I carried them with me.

There is a quiet strength in me now, a conviction to fight for the justice of worthiness in myself and others. It started with kindness. Kindness toward myself came first—because only by offering it inward could I radiate it outward. Only by believing I deserve love could I finally embrace it.

And if I could believe that for myself, then surely, humanity was worthy too.

"A PART OF US"

Yael Naim

CHAPTER 17

THE SPIRIT OF THE BIRD

For 47 years, I froze in time, encased in the amber of my history. That was until I finally broke free.

I took my power back. It was always mine to begin with, but I had forgotten. I had buried it beneath years of pain and self-doubt.

My mission was clear—to unearth the lost versions of myself buried in the rubble, forgotten and boxed away. I owed them more than remembrance. I owed them reclamation. Brick by brick, I rebuilt what had been taken—my confidence, my love, my belief in myself and more.

I sent all the abuse back to its rightful owner with a return-to-sender label. It was never mine to carry. It was theirs to own.

I gathered the fragments of myself in a quiet vigil, a sacred ceremony of remembering and restoring.

To my one-year-old self, I returned her magic—the pure, unshakable belief that she belonged in this world. That she had always been worthy of love and claiming.

To my eight-year-old, I filled a bathtub of warm water, rose petals, and solidarity. I washed away all the debris of shame, loss, and deep sadness. Dressed in a white luxurious robe to restore her innocence, she fell fast asleep in my arms listening to a bedtime story.

To the ten-year-old who watched her brother beaten while she stood frozen in helplessness, soft words layered the heartache: *You were never weak. You were the strong one. The one who survived. The one who saw his violence for what it was—a reflection of his weakness, not yours.*

To the girl who grew up hungry, uprooted, and never certain where home would be, I whispered the truth: You are safe now—more than enough food in the freezer, a haven with deep roots, and the long-awaited stability you hoped for.

To the teenager, I gave her a glimpse of her future. She once believed that sex was both a weapon and a desperate way to gain the love and attention she craved. She glimpsed her future. Love so profound that it washed away all the shadows. That was found in the family she built, in the children and the husband who loved her beyond all sense of proportion. The love she had been searching for was always there, quietly waiting. She only had to trust and hold on.

Unraveling the knots of verbal abuse required a delicate touch. After years of flinching from her own reflection, she finally paused—truly looked at herself. For the first time, she met her own dark brown eyes and let the moment stretch, no longer turning away.

In those eyes, she saw something she hadn't recognized before: potential, bravery, and a quiet softness. There was truth in that steady gaze; a reassurance she had spent an entire lifetime searching for.

I created a welcoming home, a haven where my children grew up surrounded by love and consistency. They were raised in the same house, with a deep understanding of a solid foundation.

We paid off the mortgage early, making that brick house—a cottage-like sanctuary—entirely our own. I tended the land with care, treating it as a partner, offering gratitude for everything it provided. In return, the land would nourish me, filling our lives with food, abundance and peace.

I was no longer defined by the suffocating grip of alcohol and the allure of substances that had once offered a fleeting escape and a false sense of self. In their place, happiness and balance quietly returned, bringing me closer to the person I was always meant to become.

Every story, every trauma, and every broken piece had its purpose. They had all led me to this moment. When I finally walked out of the gates of hell, as the flames flickered and danced behind me, I didn't look back.

I wiped the soot from my eyes, and I saw the truth; the universe had been waiting to make things right. The gift lay exposed, hidden in plain sight. I opened my hands, gathering every version of myself that had struggled—holding them gently, and safely within my grasp. With quiet certainty, I promised they would never be forgotten again.

Through self-discovery, I was transformed—an undeterred soul rising from the wreckage. A true survivor's story, the hero's journey. I felt love—true, unshakable love. No longer bound by the past, I soared beyond the gates of hell, my spirit ignited, and wings ablaze: powerful and free.

I rose like a thunderbird, a phoenix reborn—no longer searching, no longer lost. The fire that had once consumed me now illuminated the path forward. I became my own sanctuary, and my own salvation. I finally came home.

I did not just escape the flames—I became them. I reclaimed, redefined, and resurrected myself. This was not the end of my story. This was the beginning of everything.

"SPIRIT BIRD"

Xavier Rudd.

Special thanks for this song that helped set me free.

CHAPTER 18

FIELD NOTES: UNIVERSAL TRAVEL LESSONS

N ot all healing looks like meditating on a mountaintop. Sometimes, it looks like purging into a bucket while your soul is being turned inside out. This year-long journey—and the use of therapeutic psychedelics in a supported, intentional setting—was a world apart from the casual experimentation of my youth. It wasn't a party. It wasn't recreational. It was a deliberate commitment to deep, often painful, soul-searching work.

I committed to 365 days of healing, attending a therapeutic psychedelic ceremony every four to six weeks to confront the buried trauma I had spent decades avoiding. For years, I had hidden—from childhood trauma, abuse, addiction, low self-esteem, and more. The list of wounds was long, but so was my determination to heal.

I learned countless lessons throughout the year, and it's important to acknowledge the responsibility that came with this path.

Psychedelics aren't a quick fix, a magic cure, or something to take lightly. This is *WORK*—sacred, challenging, and deeply personal.

I was fortunate. I worked with skilled, experienced medicine practitioners who understood the weight of this work and the responsibility it carried. Their integrity helped shape my journey.

Well-intentioned practitioners are brave souls, guiding one person at a time toward healing. But their impact doesn't stop there, it ripples outward to families, communities, and, ultimately, the world. Their work is nothing short of sacred.

I traveled far and wide to seek out legalized locations for these medicines—whenever possible. This path was never taken lightly. I leveraged connections within the medicine community, interviewed multiple practitioners, and meticulously researched every step of the process. Over the course of a year, I left my home state—and the country—many times.

While these medicines hold the potential for profound healing and transformation, they must be approached with caution, respect, and deep reverence. Missteps or recklessness can cause harm—not only to the individual, but also to the forward progress of these powerful healing tools.

This brings me to the shadow side of this work.

There are "pop-up shamans" in every town, and that scares the shit out of me. These are people who often prioritize profit and ego over true healing, putting their own self-interests ahead of the collective benefit. Their recklessness endangers vulnerable people seeking help, and jeopardizes the integrity and safety of ethical, experienced practitioners.

For me, it was absolutely critical to vet the person facilitating the medicine. Before working with anyone, I sought out references from people I trusted, listened to personal stories from past participants and asked hard questions about their training, lineage, and ethics.

This work can change lives—or destroy them. The difference lies in who is running the space, set and setting.

Integration was equally important to my journey—the process of embodying the lessons, not just experiencing them. The medicine itself was only a fraction of the work—maybe 10%. The remaining 90% happened when I returned home to put into practice the lessons I learned.

In hindsight, and over the course of the year, I wish I had slowed down to give myself time to process, integrate, and breathe between ceremonies. It took almost a year to realize I should step back, work less, and allow healing to unfold naturally. I regret being a slow learner, but healing met me at my own pace.

For years, I worked in local food systems, side by side with small farmers—true stewards of the land. I watched as they moved in rhythm with the earth, carrying the quiet wisdom that comes from tending soil, coaxing life from the ground with calloused hands and boundless devotion. There is peace in the connection, an unspoken love story between human and earth—one that can be breathtaking in its beauty or brutal in its challenges. They understood, in a way that many have forgotten, that we are not separate from nature; part of our existence is owed to the air we breathe, the soil beneath our feet, and the delicate balance that sustains us all.

Recently, I read an article in which dermatologists warned against using beef tallow as a cosmetic moisturizer. The debate itself didn't faze me—what struck me was the deeper issue it represented: how disconnected society is from nature.

Western medicine has a place. Earth, in all its infinite wisdom deserves a seat at the table. It's about balance. For years, I dismissed the idea that healing could come from Earth—because it didn't have a prescription label. But psilocybin and ayahuasca challenged that belief, offering me a chance to reexamine my worldview—my relationship with nature and my place within it.

Earth became my greatest teacher, the wisest of them all. It carried millions of years of learned memory, a living archive of survival, adaptation, and renewal. And when I finally slowed down enough to listen, it showed me the missing pieces of the map guiding me to my own healing. It saved me—not with force, but with quiet, ancient wisdom, whispering the answers that had been there all along.

Prioritizing practices and environments that resonate with goodness and align with the higher vibrations of my healing journey made all the difference. About six months in, I began working with an integration therapist—a crucial space for unpacking and processing the lessons that each ceremony had revealed. By month eleven, I added an intuitive detective into the mix, someone who challenged me to dig deeper, to question my stories, my perceptions, and my deeply ingrained beliefs.

Before I began this journey, I immersed myself in research, determined to understand the potential of therapeutic psychedelics as a tool for healing trauma. But as I explored the space, I noticed something was missing—a gap in the conversation that no one seemed to be addressing.

Celebrity testimonials about psychedelic healing were popping up—stories of enlightenment, life-changing insights, and profound transformations shared on podcasts and talk shows, as well as in bestselling books. Their experiences opened the door for a broader audience, making the conversation a little more mainstream.

But I noticed stigmas still lingered, and important conversations were missing, especially in lower and middle-class America.

Everyday people—the legions living in ordinary houses, walking the dogs, stocking fridges, raising kids, and clocking into jobs quietly carrying the weight of past trauma. For many, survival means burying the stories deep, tucking them away where no one can see. To endure. To adapt. To move through life without ever acknowledging the burdens they shoulder.

As I said, no one makes small talk with the neighbors about healing through therapeutic psychedelics.

I saw the toll of hardship—the sacrifices made, and the silent suffering of broken souls in my neighborhood and work. I heard the echoes of past childhood trauma and felt the weight of their unspoken pain. I saw high suicide rates in the people who grew our food, fought for our country and countless others, a quiet battle raging beneath the surface of many conversations.

We were all moving through life together, like ghosts of our own pasts—haunted but functioning, bound by silence and the weight of unspoken truths.

I searched for stories like mine—trauma abuse survivors. People who carried their trauma quietly like a whisper on the wind of conversation yet strived for a deeper understanding in daily life.

But I couldn't find them. And that's when I realized—I had to tell my *own* story.

Most importantly, this is my story, my journey. This book is not an invitation or encouragement for others to follow the same path; it is simply a memoir, a reflection of my personal experience with healing, questioning, and growth. The choice to explore any path toward self-betterment is deeply personal. I honor and respect each person's right to choose whatever leads them back to the fullness of their being. I trust them to know what is right for themselves.

> **"WHAKAARIA MAI - HOW GREAT THOU ART"**
> *TEEKS, Hollie Smith*

CHAPTER 19

THE OTHER SIDE OF HEALING

In the end, the "buck up" life had a purpose—as it turns out, it wasn't just a fast track to emotional repression. I tackled healing the way famous podcaster Tim Ferriss tackles…well, everything—like it was the 4-Hour Healing Plan. Did I end up with a hot new body? No. Did my cooking skills improve? Also no. But the "work-week" part? That changed.

Healing became my second full-time job; one I took just as seriously as my actual paycheck. For years, "buck up" had kept me out of prison and conveniently emotionally detached, but when it was time to do the work, that no-bullshit survival mentality came in handy. I didn't mess around.

In ceremonies, they often warn you not to rush into life-altering decisions. Don't go home and immediately quit your job, divorce your spouse, or set your life on fire. Let the awakenings settle. Give them months, not moments, to see if they still hold true.

But for me, some changes couldn't wait. Nothing was impulsive, but I began to recognize that certain choices weren't just about change, they were about survival. Some meant letting go, not because I wanted to, but because I needed to. At first, it felt selfish, like a betrayal of everything I held dear for so long.

Then I realized: I can't heal myself while I am drowning. And I had been drowning for years. The only difference now was that I could finally see the shore. And for the first time, I wanted to swim toward it, pull myself onto solid ground, and step into a life with purpose.

The biggest change I made was leaving my role as the executive director of a nonprofit I had founded—an organization I had nurtured like a child, because in many ways, it was my baby. Built from the ground up with love, community, and deep purpose, it wasn't just a mission—it was an extension of my heart. For a long time, it was my dream.

I poured countless hours into it, fueled by passion—for the farmers I adored, a food system that nourished me, the land and stewards who cared for it. But my passion came at a cost. I loved my work more than I loved myself. I forgot to tend my own land. I wasn't being a good steward—not of myself, and not of my own well-being.

Extracting myself from the job was excruciating. It felt like ripping away a piece of my soul. But I finally understood I couldn't help others if I didn't save myself first. Still, the guilt weighed on me for months—until a friend said something that changed everything: "Katie, you aren't leaving them. You are leading them."

Then, a farmer said, "Katie, there are more effective ways to help these people. Use your gifts. We're all tired and struggling. You did a hell of a job with the nonprofit, but we need your help getting through our days." Those words settled in my heart, bringing a clarity I was searching for.

Years of suffering, abuse, and asking, "Why me?" eventually led to an answer: I could help others. That realization led me to start Peace & Fire Healing in Boise—not because I had everything figured out, but because I understood what it meant to walk through the fire and find peace.

I began as the wounded healer, then evolved into a reluctant healer, and, ultimately, stepped fully into the role of the intuitive healer. I don't claim to have all the answers, but I've come to understand that healing isn't about fixing—it's about guiding, holding space, and walking alongside others as they find their own way.

The struggles   the abuse, addiction, shame, and the life-altering storms—had purpose, even when I couldn't see it. The universe knew it could bend me and I wouldn't break. And in the end, there was a reason: to help others face their own shadows. And with that revelation, coupled with a new reason to live, I accepted the mission.

Life was not just something to be endured. With deep appreciation, I could engage more fully. That was so humbling, it shook my core.

Through it all, I've learned to recognize the true blessings in my days: my incredible family, my friends, and the undeniable purpose that revealed itself along the way. The hard stuff that inevitably rises each day isn't just struggle; it's a teacher.

I am not perfect—I am a human, flawed, and ever-evolving. Growth happens in the lessons, the vulnerability, and the willingness to face each new day with acceptance.

I had support, and I recognize that not everyone has that gift. I was fortunate, but I also finally *saw* the blessing. I created community and support. I did the work. Not perfectly, but I sure as hell tried.

I get the opportunity to love with a grateful heart, which feels pure, good, and right.

This journey isn't just about natural medicine. It's about the process, the people, the unfolding, and the becoming. And no one should walk it alone. Healing takes many forms—there is no one path. What humanity needs now, more than ever, is possibility and options.

Sometimes, the weight of the world feels unbearable. But this feels like a new mission: one fueled by hard-earned knowledge of how these medicines can help humanity, with a deep reverence for their power, and a hell of a lot of hope.

Thank you for taking *your* precious time to read *my* story. I am sending you so much love for your own journey. However, you navigate it, whatever path you take to get there, I believe in your possibility.

Because damn it, you deserve it.

And I know—the universe will hold your hair back.

"HYMN TO THE SOUL"

LAOR

MY RIDE OR DIES

I wouldn't be here without a village—the ones who held me when I was unraveling, who wiped my nose, dried my tears, asked about the book (again and again), and carried my heart in their cupped hands like it was something sacred.

To my children—my soul teachers. In all their profound wisdom, they became the light that led me home. For years, I buried my pain so I could show up for them, never knowing they were the ones who would ultimately show up for me. My son's words at the firepit were all true. This path of healing began with baby steps, and in their fierce and quiet grace, they walked beside me until I could walk it alone.

They listened while I read chapters aloud—my trauma laid bare, piece by piece, over the course of a year. And they held me through it with nothing but love. My son was right—it *was* my turn and they had my back. And they made sure I took it. Ella and Dylan, you are and will always be the reason I find the strength to face each day. Loving you helped me find my way back to loving myself. And for that, I am eternally grateful and so dang proud to be your mom.

And you know how parents always hope their kids end up with good people? Mine did. Two incredible humans—kind, grounded, and full of light. I'm so grateful you're part of the crew. The artwork on the website was created by my son's wife, Taylor. My daughter's partner, Max, lent his editing skills to this book. In every way, this was a family endeavor.

To my husband—your support, your unwavering love, and your belief in me are unmatched. You gave me exactly what I needed, moment by moment, without question or hesitation. A true healer, not by training but by the nature of your heart—kind, steady, and pure. I married my soulmate, and after more than 30 years, we're still laughing at ourselves, being silly as hell, and choosing joy, over and over again. Thank you for giving so much of yourself to everyone around you. Your footprint touches the world in quiet, extraordinary ways.

To my mom—you listened for hours. I mean *hours*. You are the wisest of souls, and the hurting seem to find their way to you like moths to light. Through everything we've been through, we've found healing not just for ourselves, but for our family—and through that, we've sent that healing back into the world. You are the original shortie badass, in all the best ways.

And Steve—thank you for giving our relationship grace, patience, and room to grow. Through honest conversations and shared challenges, we found our way. Thank you for showing up, for evolving with me, and for being a dad in the truest, most grounded sense of the word.

To my brother, C (Mike)—what a big, bold life we've lived together. Through the chaos and the beauty, I am so honored to be your sister. You've been one of the greatest blessings of my life.

T (Tommy)—your good heart and mine beat as one. Your love is innocent, steady, and a gift I carry with me always. K (Billy), I know you're up in heaven, but I felt you were with me in every chapter of this book. Your spirit sat beside me, steady and quiet, as if reminding me to keep going. Thank you for being close.

Marilyn Isaac—thank you for seeing the light in me and offering your lens to capture it. You made me feel seen and beautiful during a vulnerable time, and that's no small thing.

Much love to all the wonderful humans in my life. You bring richness, honesty, humility, and strength to my journey. I am a better human because you are in it.

And to you—dear (ones) reader, thank you for walking this path with me. Whether you're here to understand, to heal, or simply to feel less alone, know this: you are not broken. You are becoming.

And to Spirit—the great mystery that held me when I forgot how to hold myself—thank you for gently, relentlessly guiding me back to forgiveness, hope, love, and a true sense of home. You whispered the words I needed, again and again, until I could finally whisper them to myself.

And to Earth—my oldest, wisest friend. None of this would have been possible without you. You waited, so patiently, for me to remember you. And I did.

Hands held. Spirit whispered. Earth waited.

And I remembered.

"LITTLE GIANT"

Roo Panes

ABOUT THE AUTHOR

Katie Baker is a writer, advocate, and childhood abuse survivor who has transformed her journey of trauma and healing into a story of resilience, empowerment, and hope. After years of battling addiction, shame, and the lingering effects of a tumultuous childhood, she found profound transformation through therapeutic psychedelics, deep inner work, and spiritual exploration.

In her memoir, *When The Universe Holds Your Hair Back*, Katie shares her raw and deeply personal journey—a story of confronting the past, reclaiming lost parts of herself, and embracing a life of authenticity, self-love, and purpose. Through candid storytelling, she offers readers a path toward healing and the courage to face their own darkness with grace.

Now an intuitive energy healer, speaker, and mentor, Katie assists others in breaking free from generational pain, reconnecting with their true selves, and stepping into their power. She is passionate about integrating ancient wisdom, modern healing modalities, and the power of psychedelics to guide others toward profound personal transformation.

When she's not writing or working with clients, Katie finds joy in cultivating her garden, growing her own food, taking long walks with her beloved dogs, and cherishing time with her incredible family and friends.

BOOKS, BEATS & BEYOND

If this book stirred something inside you—if you're carrying pain, grief, or a quiet knowing that it's time to heal—please know that you're not alone. My story is just one of many. **Yours matters too.**

Whether you're curious about my journey updates, exploring energy healing, navigating integration, or simply trying to find your way back to yourself, I'm here to support the next chapter of your path.

STAY CONNECTED

Join the monthly(ish) Dandelion Resistance newsletter.

Because damn it, we're not weeds—we grow in the cracks because we're resilient as hell.

What you'll get:

- Healing updates (because this is a lifelong process, and there's no shortage of content)

- Playlists, book and TV recs that support the soul

- News on upcoming groups and future books

- Real, raw stories and grounded inspiration

Sign up at: **peaceandfirehealing.com/newsletter**

LISTEN ALONG

Check out the **official book playlist**—the songs that carried me through the hardest and most beautiful moments of healing.

Search *Peace & Fire Healing—When The Universe Holds Your Hair Back* on Spotify, or scan the QR code:

SPREAD THE LIGHT

If this book resonated with you:

- Leave a review on Amazon or Goodreads

- Follow Peace & Fire Healing on social—links are on the
  website: **peaceandfirehealing.com**

- Tell a friend who might need this story

Want to explore more? Scan the QR code to visit the book's earth
home base—*When The Universe Holds Your Hair Back.*

www.ingramcontent.com/pod-product-compliance
Lightning Source LLC
Chambersburg PA
CBHW021223130626
46554CB00004B/1340